Procurement Reengineering

Ben Laaper

PT Publications, Inc.
P.O. Box 310266
Miami, Florida 33131

Library of Congress Cataloging-in-Publication Data

Laaper, Ben, 1951-
Procurement reengineering / Ben Laaper
p. cm.
Includes bibliographic references and index.
ISBN 0-945456-31-X (pbk.)
1. Industrial procurement. 2. Reengineering (Management)
3. Electronic data interchange I. Title.
HD39.5.L3 1997
658.7'2--dc21 97-40468
CIP

Second Printing - December 2001

Printed in the United States of America

Table of Contents

ABOUT THE AUTHOR
Ben H. Laaper C.P.M. & CPIM

Ben Laaper is the Director, Materials & Purchasing for Accuride Corporation in Henderson, Kentucky. Previously, he worked for DSM Engineering Plastics both in Reading, Pennsylvania and Evansville, Indiana. He has been in the forefront of reengineering the procurement process for quite some time. He has conducted seminars and workshops in Purchasing and Materials Management related areas at Penn State, IUPUI and the University of Southern Indiana.

He is past president of the Central Pennsylvania Chapter of the National Association of Purchasing Management and a frequent after-dinner speaker at both the NAPM and APICS local chapters. He was a presenter at the 1996 NAPM International Purchasing Conference in Chicago.

Ben is a native from The Netherlands and emigrated to the United States upon his graduation from college. He can be reached by email at: blaaper@evansville.net

How to Use this Book

This book is designed to be used in conjunction with the corollary texts in our Purchasing Series. Please call us at the number below for more information about utilizing our tools. The idea behind this book is to read it with a pen in your hand so that you can answer the questions and write down the plans you are going to put into action. For those people who use this book alone, there is enough information to get you started on the road to excellence. Remember, however, that roadmaps such as this book are best accompanied by travel guides such as the ones we offer in the field of purchasing. Together, they can make your journey a rewarding one.

HELP DESK HOTLINE
1-800-547-4326

In order to answer the questions of our readers, we have established a Help Desk Hotline at our corporate headquarters in West Palm Beach, Florida. We invite you to call us with your queries about how to use the forms and tools in this book.

We also invite you to use our HELP DESK HOTLINE to find out more about other books we publish, as well as our *Supplier Surveys and Audits Forms* software and a videotape series entitled **Supplier Certification: The Path to Excellence**. In addition to books, software and videotapes, we offer over 80 courses which can be scheduled for intensive, in-house seminars. Call us for details.

Change and More Change

Chapter One

1.1 Fasten Your Seat Belt

In spite of great intentions, lots of momentum, hundreds of business articles and numerous books on the subject, many companies continue to flounder at "Reengineering the Corporation." It seems that many organizations are just waiting for the "Magic Wand of Reengineering" to strike while others have made serious attempts but failed to get the desired results because they either refrained from aggressively reorganizing for change, attempted to tackle too many processes simultaneously, or allowed for certain isolated functions to remain independent.

Reengineering requires top management support but above all else - leadership - since most projects are focused on revenue generating and value-adding processes such as business growth, customer order realization and lead time reductions. Contrary to popular belief, reengineering doesn't have to encompass all aspects of a business at once but can be performed within certain, independent, closed-loop processes. Departments in and by themselves cannot be reengineered because they merely represent a component of a process and not a process in its entirety. A process, on the other hand, runs across numerous functional areas and departments. An example of such a cross-functional process is the procurement process which, inasmuch as it touches every employee, is a process that is self-contained between the requisitioner, Purchasing, Receiving and Accounts Payable. It also is a process that, traditionally speaking, consists of numerous poorly coordinated silo types of functions and controls.

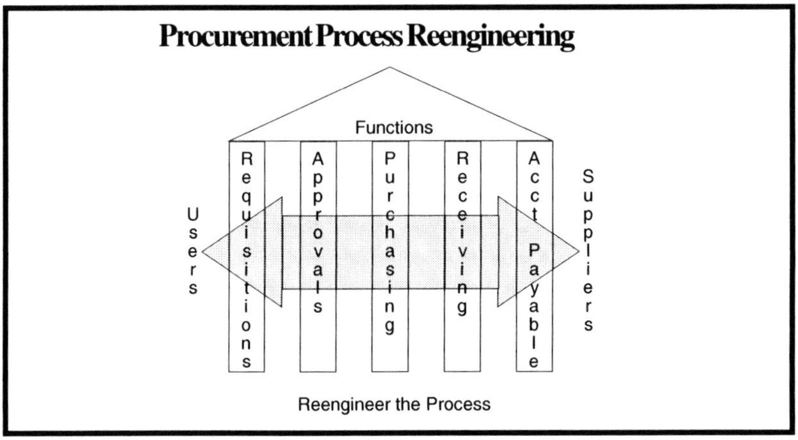

Figure 1.1

In subsequent generations of reengineering many companies and Business Process experts have come to the realization that the procurement process in particular, offers substantial opportunities, as it appears to consist of very expensive, bureaucratic and non-value-adding activities. For companies seeking continuous optimization and true cost reductions, the procurement process by and in itself is considered "low hanging fruit," one of the last great bastions of major inefficiencies yet to be conquered. Once reengineered, the entire procurement process should, through the process of empowerment and decentralization, simulate the Total Quality Management movement, which ultimately makes all the operators and process owners accountable for quality and the cost of quality. It took approximately a decade, starting in the early 1980s, and beginning with Statistical Process Control, for the quality culture to be fully integrated into our processes. Now, through procurement process Reengineering, we appear to be on the eve of another cultural breakthrough: the decentralization of and a substantial reduction in the cost of acquisition. The cost of quality ranged from 15-18% of a company's total costs just a decade ago, compared to less than 5% of total costs for today's world class companies. Similarly, the cost of procurement and acquisition should tumble from 6% of today's total costs to less than 2% over the next few years. As it turns out it is the process in itself that is cost prohibitive, or to paraphrase then presidential candidate Bill Clinton: "It is the process, Idiot!"

Some of the more obvious costs associated with the procurement process include:

- maintaining a larger than needed supplier base.
- obtaining larger than needed volumes.
- lack of standardization.
- the cost of extended lead times and cycle times.
- the cost of order processing & receiving.

Unfortunately, beyond a few strategic raw material suppliers the executive level interest in Purchasing drops off faster than it took the Allied Forces to crush the Iraqi resistance in the Gulf War. This is not only unfortunate, but also a very expensive short coming in the way our corporations are managed, as many companies still treat the purchases of shop supplies as some sort of black magic. Traditional purchasing organizations are quite isolated and continue to hang onto a set of outdated policies and procedures that call for extensive bidding cycles. This kind of bureaucracy tends to perpetuate variability in: product, process and service along with increased lead times and cycle times.

Consequently, this should no longer abdicate the procurement professional from seriously taking a close look at how the often voluminous and bureaucratic purchasing process functions, or, as it turns out, dysfunctions, within the majority of our corporations. Even today, as we rapidly approach the 21st century, we find the traditional, auction type, purchasing process still at work in at least 75% of all companies. Even at divisions and plant locations of many Fortune 100 corporations, we still encounter such elaborate, outdated, non-value-adding systems. Consider this example from an international pharmaceutical company. When its maintenance department needed some fasteners, it followed all the proper procedures. That resulted in a long-distance phone call, a fax, and a two part purchase order—all for a $2.18 box of fasteners. Many routine maintenance items are purchased in such an elaborate and expensive fashion.

1.2 Why Purchasing?

In spite of the overwhelming evidence to the contrary, most procurement professionals have a very difficult time in breaking away from their customary cycle of doing business the old fashioned way and often don't possess the leadership skills to break out of the mold to bring about true radical change. However, purchasing is the key component within the procurement process, and it must help drive the elimination of paper work and the facilitation of the migration of transactions to sources external to the organization. In order to optimize a company's performance the Chief Executives and Business Process experts need to aggressively focus on the need for partnerships and alliances throughout the entire organization. It is not the high profile raw materials that absorb the cost of acquisition but the basic shop supplies, referred to throughout this book as Maintenance, Repair and Operating supplies (MRO).

When we refer to Reengineering the procurement process, we must realize that in most traditional companies the accounting control process in fact functions as an imposed purchasing process. Therefore, through reengineering we are seeking for the emergence of an entirely new identity for Purchasing. This new identity should be the catalyst to turn the department upside-down and create a new process where Purchasing rapidly gains credibility and enables it to flourish by getting into areas heretofore inaccessible to purchasing personnel.

1.3 Purchasing - The Narrow Focus

In the great race toward economic power and competitive advantage, successful companies are constantly looking to permanently reduce their costs. Purchasing personnel, on the other hand, have been trained to go after the lowest price regardless of total costs because within its functional silo capacity no visibility nor accountability exists that exposes any external cost inhibitors.

Many traditional purchasing departments still struggle with the concepts of single and sole sourcing versus multiple sourcing. For the record, single sourcing is buying from one source exclusively by design, whereas sole sourcing is buying from one source exclusively due to the lack of any other options. The threat of single sourcing is often unfounded as purchasing professionals often fail to recognize that true supplier partnerships and supplier integration at all levels of the organization can often lead to substantial reductions in total costs. Furthermore, many single source supplier programs could be duplicated fairly rapidly if the need arises.

In the past, Purchasing has limited its focus to three very basic commodities:

- Maintenance, Repair & Operating supplies (MRO)
- Standard and specialty manufacturing components

- Raw materials (often with the exception of strategic or high dollar-value materials)

In doing so, Purchasing has missed the boat in adding value to, or even being in the decision-making loop of, the more upscale services. As a matter of fact, a 1995 study by CAPS, the Center for Advanced Purchasing Studies [the research arm the National Association of Purchasing Management (NAPM)] found that only 41% of an organization's dollars are spent by the purchasing department. According to CAPS, this is primarily the result of Purchasing's very limited involvement in the more upscale, nontraditional purchases such as utilities, leasing, health care, insurance and travel.

1.4 The Paper Work Monster

Because of its outsider status, Purchasing relies heavily on, and is very preoccupied with, its lifeline into the organization "the requisition and paper flow process." Consequently, traditional purchasing departments don't have the clout necessary to participate in, let alone manage, important business criteria. This is fueled by the fact that upscale purchases and services, such as utilities, normally don't require a requisition or purchase order, thus avoiding the traditional process all together.

In its functional role, Purchasing was driven and controlled by the accounting department, namely the controller. It functioned as the watchdog for old-style bookkeepers, often putting itself out on the limb in helping to divide and allocate mundane commodities such as office supplies, spare parts and paper goods. The traditional methods of buying are not only cumbersome and outdated, but also excessively expensive to maintain. Did you ever wonder what is meant when you are told: "It costs my company $75 to issue a purchase order." Or what it means as the W. W. Grainger company advertises: "How the $17 hammer ended up costing the company $100." Obviously the point is that price is often only a fraction of the total cost. The balance largely consists of non-value-added administrative paper work!

1.5 Speed: The New Paradigm of the 1990s

After World War II, the United States found itself in an almost monopolistic position: it was the only country that had an industrial base left standing. However, by the early 1980s the United States was experiencing tough competition in the global manufacturing arena. It appeared that Far Eastern competition, most notably Japan, had attacked the marketplace through a new angle called quality. We quickly learned through consumer preferences that there was no trade-off between cost and quality. As a result, a massive quality movement arose across the United States as many companies embraced the Total Quality Management concept. Our new environment requires Purchasing to be much more fluid and focus on value-adding activities.

This competitive threat brought about a certain survival perspective that helped us sharpen our skills and desire to be the undisputed global economic engine once more. Driven by a thriving service economy, we developed a passion for customer satisfaction and excellence. This paradigm shift happened in the early 1990s. By competing on speed we should be able to score improvements in both quality and cost while simultaneously reducing our lead times.

The emergence of global markets and the advent of ever improving Information Technology (IT) have drastically leveled the playing field for almost all market leaders. Companies that can either drive or respond very effectively to changing market dynamics are in the best position to survive, or better yet, thrive in the new economic world order.

1.6 What's the Impact of Speed Upon Purchasing?

In order to not only support but also drive the entire movement toward speed, Purchasing must reinvent itself, downsize and transform from a function into a process, or better yet, a seamless process. When redesigned properly the new process will rapidly communicate needs, changes and enhancements between the company and its suppliers. To reinvent the department, however, purchasing personnel must examine their mission and thoroughly understand Supply Chain Management and the difference between the basic concepts of purchasing and buying, concepts which have become blurred over time. Whereas Purchasing should be concerned with the strategic planning aspects of the procurement process, buying in itself deals with the execution of daily transactions and replenishment - actions which should be performed as closely to a company's end user as possible. Consequently, sourcing or procurement marketing, the process of developing partnerships and strategic alliances needs to become organizationally divorced from the buying process. Sourcing is a strategic process which needs to be within a "Matrix" organizational position, where its members participate in numerous cross-functional teams with Marketing, Research & Development, Engineering, Production and Quality Assurance. The actual buying process, this is the part that must be seamless, should be performed at the plant or consumption level in a redesigned process that is void of paper and which facilitates direct supplier integration, where practical, with the requisitioner or end user.

1.7 The Origin and Application of Reengineering

Reengineering the procurement process may not have the same dynamic marketing appeal as, for example, "Reengineering the Corporation" developed by and based on the book written by Michael Hammer and James Champy.

Provided the reengineering team recognizes procurement as a core or key Business Process, and is supported by top management, Business Process Reengineering (BPR) should have a profound and liberating impact on the entire organization. Purchasing could yet become the true champion in becoming a process-driven organization. After all, every company or institution, no matter how big or small, performs some type of procurement function and every individual within those organizations consumes some type of goods, services or supplies. Yet, just about every company struggles as to how these purchases are actually made, how they are received, how they are accounted for and how they get paid. Some companies employ all kinds of systems and methods often resulting in an Accounts Payable nightmare. The new era of empowerment has in fact fueled this situation as more and more employees "do their own thing" in obtaining supplies. This has brought about the following highly undesirable scenarios:

- An often uncontrollable invoice reconciliation process
- A major departure from product standardization
- A proliferation of suppliers
- A loss of pricing control
- Diluted purchasing leverages

Consequently, in traditional and many newly empowered organizations, the purchasing/accounts payable process is highly disconnected and in shambles, making it an ideal candidate for reengineering.

1.8 Alternate Processes

Some companies, in an overreaction to the "Purchasing Monster" have armed legions of its people with procurement or credit cards. While procurement cards are a great tool in transforming a company and in reducing the procurement cycle time, they could, when no limits or controls are designed into such a program, cause more pain than benefit as everyone becomes his own buyer, expediter and controller. Just launching a procurement card program without design merely transfers all the non-value-added activities from Purchasing and Accounts Payable to the front office and the factory floor ... a far cry from reengineering.

Again, when used properly, procurement cards play a critical role in the "new" purchasing process, but more in terms of an integral part of a better defined "new" process. (See Chapter 5.8 for further details.) The new purchasing process must be paperless where possible and legally acceptable but it also must be comprehensible and represent the overall best value to the company.

The president and CEO of a Pennsylvania-based, second tier automotive supplier, ABC Manufacturing, Inc., called for a major reengineering campaign after she learned of the cost of the acquisition process. She learned that all the raw materials purchased by her company represented 89.5% or $175,000,000 of all purchases which were contracted from only seven suppliers and handled by two individuals. Through supplier partnerships and use of Supply Chain Management and Electronic Data Interchange a virtually paperless system was developed through which inventories were controlled very effectively.

The purchasing and control of the Maintenance, Repair & Operating (MRO) supplies which made up most of the remaining 10.5% or approximately $20,000,000 was a totally different story. The MRO purchases where handled by a staff of nine people who collectively processed more than 35,000 requisitions and 15,000 purchase orders annually. These numbers represented only the front-end of a massive and gigantic paper trail. "What's wrong with this picture?" the president questioned the organization.

The primary objectives for the reengineering team were to:

- create a closed-loop process from requisitioning through invoice payment.

- reduce the supplier base from more than 2,000 to less than 100 suppliers.
- reduce the cost of the procurement process by at least 50%.
- standardize equipment and processes where possible.
- aggressively reduce cycle times.
- eliminate paper work.
- educate, train, reorganize and restructure the organization to reflect the new process.

The reengineering campaign was hugely successful and took nearly 18 months to fully implement and evolve. The key success factor was the development of partnerships with a handful of MRO suppliers which captured nearly 80% of all the transactions through a process called Integrated Supply— the shop's equivalent to Supply Chain Management.

In addition to these Integrated Supply relationships, ABC Manufacturing, Inc. also entered into partnerships with 18 specialty OEM-type suppliers for equipment replacement parts and committed to service contracts with another 54 suppliers to cover activities ranging from lawn maintenance to repair services, all with prenegotiated pricing, detailed call-off procedures and monthly consolidated invoicing whereby the supplier is responsible for the proof of delivery. All remaining purchases were covered by procurement cards.

In addition to the impressive progress that is being made by some industrial companies, there is one industry in particular that provides us with a clear path— the supermarket industry. Surely you have noticed the hyperactivity in your local supermarket between 7:00 -11:00 a.m. as the bread, the cola, the pretzel and the potato chip suppliers, among others, restock "their shelves." No requisitions have been issued, no purchase order has been cut, and no bureaucracy is required to restock the inventory. Why? Because the negotiations and preplanning took place much earlier in the game when well orchestrated discussions determined how much shelf space each supplier and its competitors were allotted and at what price. The actual restocking of these shelves is merely an execution of these plans. To close the loop, all the delivery person leaves behind is a signed delivery sheet for the eventual invoice reconciliation.

Supermarkets historically have coped with very tight profit margins and could ill afford an industrial-type purchasing bureaucracy. Such a process would either result in financial losses or a consumer revolt if supermarkets attempted to pass such inefficiencies down the "food chain." Integrated Supply is a further refinement upon the success enjoyed by the supermarket industry.

1.9 The New Process

The traditional (one size fits all) procurement process which historically has treated all purchases alike will in fact be replaced by four separate subprocesses depending on the application and will be customer driven. These processes are:

- Supply Chain Management ➔ Raw Materials
- Contract Management ➔ Capital Equipment
- Service Contracts ➔ Service & Utilities
- Integrated Supply ➔ MRO Supplies

Again the focus of this book will be on bestowing the philosophies and lessons learned in Supply Chain Management upon Integrated Supply and Contract Management, the area that traditionally absorbs 80% of the resources.

1.10 What Is Integrated Supply?

Integrated Supply is a Single Source Agreement for a specific commodity between a supplier and a customer whereby the supplier fully integrates itself into the customer's organization in providing products and services on demand while simultaneously merging all transactions into a single process within a paperless environment.

1.11 Outsourcing of High-Volume, Low-Value Purchases: A Paradigm Shift

At the beginning of the Industrial Revolution, emerging manufacturing companies were almost exclusively vertically integrated to guarantee the availability of raw materials, basic tools and supplies. Distribution of goods was very limited due to a lack of market infrastructure. Throughout the 20th century, however, we have seen materials and supplies become the lifeblood of industry. **Materials now make up the lion's share of most company's product cost as the purchasing content has sharply increased while the percentage of labor content has decreased correspondingly**. The specialization of labor and increased technologies makes it often more economical to buy rather than make a product. Systems integration has been a key success factor for those suppliers who offer complete assemblies (systems) instead of just components.

As our companies focus on their core competencies they come to the realization that the purchasing of Maintenance, Repair and Operating supplies (MRO) is certainly not one of them but in fact a very expensive distraction from their real purpose. For that matter, **purchases of high-volume, low-value supplies should be outsourced to and managed by system integrators.**

1.12 Total Quality Management Vs. Reengineering

On the surface it appears that Total Quality Management (TQM) and reengineering have much in common and in fact they do because they both are process focused, utilize teams, emphasize shared values and use similar tools for solving problems. TQM however, tends to be more oriented toward problem solving and optimizing certain functions, one at a time. Reengineering on the other hand, defines the boundaries of a process and eliminates all functions that constrain the process by challenging process fundamentals and their very existence. **Why, for example, are requisitions required? To satisfy an outdated auditing procedure? To launch a Purchase Order? To formally receive products? To direct the flow of receipts? None of these functions make much sense, nor add value "so let's challenge and attack the entire requisition process."**

Continuous Improvement will provide incremental functional steps forward but could be too little too late if the company is far behind the market leader and/or if it is an unprofitable enterprise. Reengineering, on the other hand, better provides quantum leap improvements.

Figure 1.2 demonstrates some of the important differences between the Total Quality Management (TQM) approach and reengineering. The TQM-driven Continuous Improvement Programs have been around for some time now and numerous companies have done very well and have truly come full circle in nurturing a culture which is highly quality conscious. Unfortunately, however, most companies have difficulties sustaining long-term interest and focus in anything that resembles a program. In fact they keep struggling with the various approaches toward manufacturing including how to deal with and how to sustain employee empowerment, self-directed work teams and a salaried work force. Reengineering will enable companies to break through this cycle of indecision because of the radical process changes it will embark upon. However, companies that have developed a strong TQM culture are more likely to succeed in reengineering because of the problem-solving attitude that has developed within such companies.

FACTORS	TQM	REENGINEERING
Type of change	Evolutionary - A better way to compete	Revolutionary - A better way of doing business
Method	Adds value to existing process	Challenges process fundamentals and their very existence
Scope	Encompasses entire organization	Focuses on core business processes
Role of technology	Traditional support	Use as enabler

Figure 1.2 Fundamental Differences Between TQM and Reengineering
Source: Best Practices in Reengineering, *David Carr and Henry Johansson, McGraw Hill, 1995, Copyright Coopers & Lybrand.*

1.13 Empowerment

The TQM approach has enabled most organizations to thwart the autocratic management style most our industries were subjected to prior to the 1980s and have moved away from such a traditional environment towards a team concept whereby employees have been empowered.

When empowerment first gained favor, many purchasing organizations were challenged because now all of a sudden every employee became an expert, always able to buy something "cheaper." The negative connotation here being the fact that requisitioners or end users equate a lower price with a lower cost. Running out for an extended lunch and treating the department to some low priced office supplies from the recently opened super discount store may superficially look like a good deal, but compared to an integrated supplier who delivers directly to the requisitioner's desk, it may prove to be an expensive and in the long term unmanageable undertaking. **In Purchasing's new role it will be tasked with bundling this new found source of enthusiasm into attractive agreements with the necessary input from critical end users.**

1.14 Cultural Change

Successful companies embrace change and will try to get ahead of the curve by seeking change to get or stay ahead of the competition, to keep the competition off balance or to continuously reduce costs from their products and/or process.

Change without cultural change is achievable in rapid fashion, but is not profound and not sustainable as it puts an organization in a state of confusion. Real change is painful by definition and will take lots of nurturing, patience and reinforcement. We should recognize that cultural change requires time to evolve. To deny this would be an insult to those affected, almost implying that one has no culture.

Radical change requires all the aforementioned but also a new approach, a new process, a renewed organization, fewer procedures and a new environment that is self-directing and designed to take a different path.

1.15 The Benefits of Reengineering the Procurement Process

Reengineering will bring about a cultural revolution, which will enable us to become more customer and process focused. Rather than being tied to the Accounting Department, Purchasing will serve as the vital link between the company and its strategic business partners - its suppliers. Through these new processes such as Supply Chain Management and Integrated Supply, Purchasing will now become responsible for:

- Technical Innovation
- Reduced Internal Cycle Times
- Reduced Purchasing Lead Times
- Improved Productivity
- Increased Quality
- Improved Customer Service
- Cost Control

Benefits Within the Procurement Arena:

- Dramatic reduction in cycle time for purchasing
- Dramatic reduction in total procurement costs
- Optimizing of all departmental activities
- Elimination of paper work
- Liberate staff to perform value-adding activities
- Concentration on customer-focused activities

Step-by-step details on how to achieve these benefits are covered in Chapter Six.

1.16 Reorganizing for Reengineering

Once the procurement process has been reengineered the organization must be radically changed in order for the process to be one continuous ongoing closed loop process. Buyers will need to be upgraded, educated and trained in their new roles while Accounts Payable must permanently become integrated in the process. The single most important aspect however, is that the old functions are disconnected and the people reassigned because otherwise, if left alone, they will revert to what they have always done before.....

1.17 Summary

Upper management is finally coming to the realization that the traditional procurement process is cost prohibitive and highly ineffective in itself. In particular shop and plant commodities such as Maintenance, Repair and Operating supplies (MRO) tend to absorb most of the purchasing resources. Consequently business leaders and business process experts consider this area "virgin territory." In reengineering the procurement process, purchasing professionals finally have an opportunity to rid themselves of the often nagging reams of paper and non-value-adding bureaucratic activities and controls. In elevating the heretofore multifunctional procurement process into a continuous closed-looped process purchasing can now help direct the migration of transactions to suppliers performing as business partners through a process called Integrated Supply. Once reengineered purchasing professionals can learn to be exactly that "professionals" and now aspire the control over upscale purchases such as utilities, insurance, leasing and outsourcing. Among the many benefits of reengineering, the focus on adding value and the dramatic reduction in total procurement cost should have a profound impact.

Acknowledgments:

Best Practices in Reengineering, David Car & Henry Johansson. McGraw Hill, 1995.

The Traditional Process

Chapter Two

2.1 Purchasing or Accounting Process

It's imperative that we have a thorough understanding of the purpose of the traditional process methods prior to reengineering. Once the entire traditional procurement cycle is subjected to process mapping, it will become clear how truly cumbersome and bureaucratic it is. (See Figure 2.1 on the next page.)

Looking at Figure 2.1, this highly confusing flow chart illustrates why the traditional process is so labor intensive and expensive to maintain. However, cumbersome and non-value-adding as it may be, traditional methods, with a similar paper distribution, are still prevalent in about 75% of our domestic companies and undoubtedly to an even higher degree in many foreign markets. Primarily small to mid-sized companies, those in the range of $25-$250MM, appear to fall

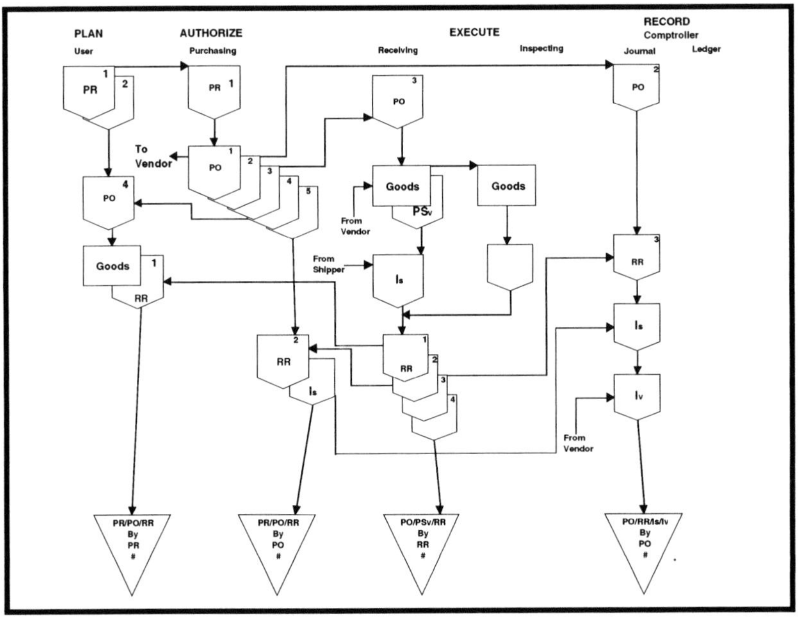

Figure 2.1. The Traditional Process Flow Chart

into this trap. Most companies actually employ advanced planning and communications methods such as Supplier Scheduling and Supply Chain Management for their raw materials acquisition. Yet the majority of these companies either have an exclusively traditional system or no system in place whatsoever when it comes to the acquisition of Maintenance, Repair and Operating supplies (MRO), despite the fact that this category often takes up more than 80% of a typical purchasing department's activities. Furthermore, the entire method of traditional purchasing is so control-oriented that once implemented, it seems to feed of itself and grow indefinitely, absorbing multi-supplier tiers along the way, resulting in a diminishing level of control or no control at all, just lots of busy work.

In as much as the initial intention may have been noble, to keep everyone honest that is, in practice the concept of verification is entirely non-value-adding. In fact the real reason for such control systems has become one of total distrust of employees and suppliers alike. This culture of distrust not only manifests itself in Purchasing, but throughout the entire procurement process, including anyone within the system who has contact with suppliers or who manages or controls any type of product movement or inventory. Yet, this behavior is not only expensive and counterproductive, it is most certainly a contradiction to the direction in which many of our companies have focused their efforts in Total Quality Management and employee empowerment process. The quality movement has given a great deal of latitude and accountability to the production worker by giving him the right to shut down a production or assembly line if the process trends out of control. Yet, on the same token we often treat these same production workers like little children when it comes to providing access to the inexpensive supply items needed to keep our processes moving along. Recently a production worker in a plastics compounding plant commented: "After all the TQM training and expensive workshops we participated in, I find it most humiliating that my company has hired somebody to guard the pipe fittings and other basic supplies I need to keep my equipment running."

2.2 Traditional Purchasing Department Activities

The daily activities in a traditional purchasing department consist almost exclusively of clerical activities which must be maintained to keep the process alive. In as much as these functional tasks are non-value-adding, they cannot just simply be dropped since all the individual functions collectively make up the process - as defunct as the process may be. Skipping certain individual steps will make the process incomplete and will result in much more work in the long run. Therefore, discarding the traditional process through layoffs and downsizing will have quite a negative effect as it increases the work load for those remaining in functional positions. In turn, this leads to a great deal of frustration and bad morale - often resulting in a further erosion of the company's financial situation. To reverse such erosion, companies will often abandon their reengineering efforts and end up restaffing as the work needs to get done. The key is making the work go away through reengineering. However, in spite of this, most companies continue to support the traditional process which, within the purchasing arena, consists of non-value-adding, functional silo steps as detailed in Figure 2.2.

Traditional Purchasing Department Activities

Process/Shuffle Papers	= 35%
Expedite Orders	= 15%
Obtain Quotations/ Auction	= 15%
Place Orders	= 15%
Receive Visitors	= 10%
Dispute/Correct Invoices	= 5%
Negotiations	= 4%
Visit Supplier Sites	= 1%

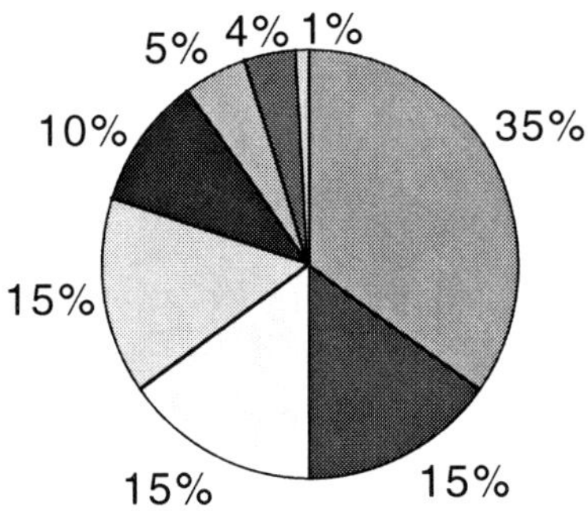

Figure 2.2

As you can see, these activities deal with reactionary, passed down, nonsynchronized functions. It is highly paper work-control-oriented (clerical) in nature and does not add value. In turn, each function or department will pass large volumes of paper work down the pipeline to the next victim - the Accounts Payable clerk whose job it is to reconcile copies of the purchase order with receiving reports, packing slips and supplier invoices, i.e. three-way matching.

Because of the sheer volume of work, a comparatively large clerical staff can be found in Accounts Payable departments that support a traditional buying organization. Sometimes it may be as high as one clerk for every $10MM in purchases and expenses whereas, in a reengineered procurement process each individual Accounts Payable clerk may support as much as $75MM to $100MM in purchases and expenses.

2.3 Reengineered Purchasing Process Activities

The reengineered procurement process looks vastly different in that it reflects the purchasing departments new role - the participation in a process that links the user with the supplier. Purchasing takes the high road in that it actively seeks to manage the supplier partnerships from a more macro position and is now more preoccupied with facilitating the process and assuring that all established metrics can be attained. The new process requires a more educated and more sophisticated buyer who will perform the activities as outlined in Figure 2.3.

Reengineered Purchasing Department Activities

Manage Contracts = 50%
(External/Internal)

Receive Visitors = 20%

Negotiations = 15%

Visit Supplier Sites = 15%

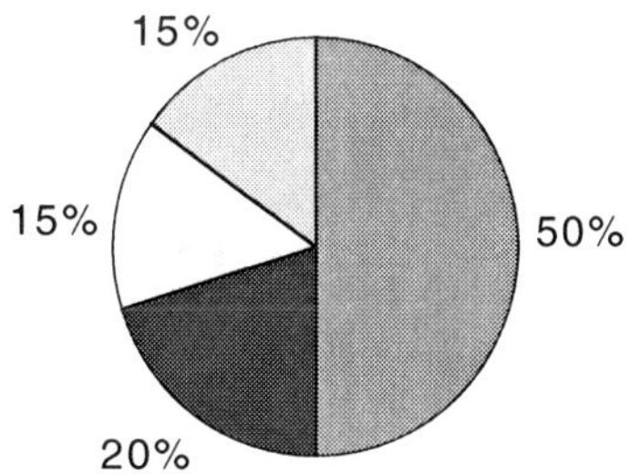

Figure 2.3

2.4 The Requisition/Approval Process

In traditional companies the approval process to replenish a supply or repair part can be very demeaning and controlling. Take a look, for example, at a screw machine shop within a manufacturing plant. With the drive toward quicker set-up reductions and efficiency improvements, equipment supplies such as perishable tools and processing aides should be located within the manufacturing cell. Yet, within the majority of companies the actual production worker spends considerable time obtaining basic supplies. In spite of much improved plant layouts and substantial reduction in cycle time, too many plant managers and production supervisors continue to use supplies as a tool to control their work force. Or, is it simply a matter of trust or fear that some supplies will "walk?" Within an empowered organization however, trust lies at the cornerstone of a company's success.

2.5 Cost of Ownership

With so much emphasis on cash flow as a business performance metric, the cost of carrying inventory has become a point of contention in many organizations. Managing these inventories tightly has become a matter of survival for many organizations as inventory can represent up to 30% of an organization's total "investments." In fact, carrying inventory is expensive, with direct costs averaging nearly 24% per annum, or 2% per month, of the value of the inventory. Five major elements make up these costs in the following manner:

Opportunity costs	=	12 to 20%
Insurance costs	=	2 to 4%
Property taxes	=	1 to 3%
Storage costs	=	1 to 3%
Obsolescence & deterioration	=	4 to 10%
Total carrying costs	=	20 to 40%

A brief overview of these carrying costs follows:

Opportunity Costs of Invested Funds. When a company buys $100,000 worth of materials it is done with funds that

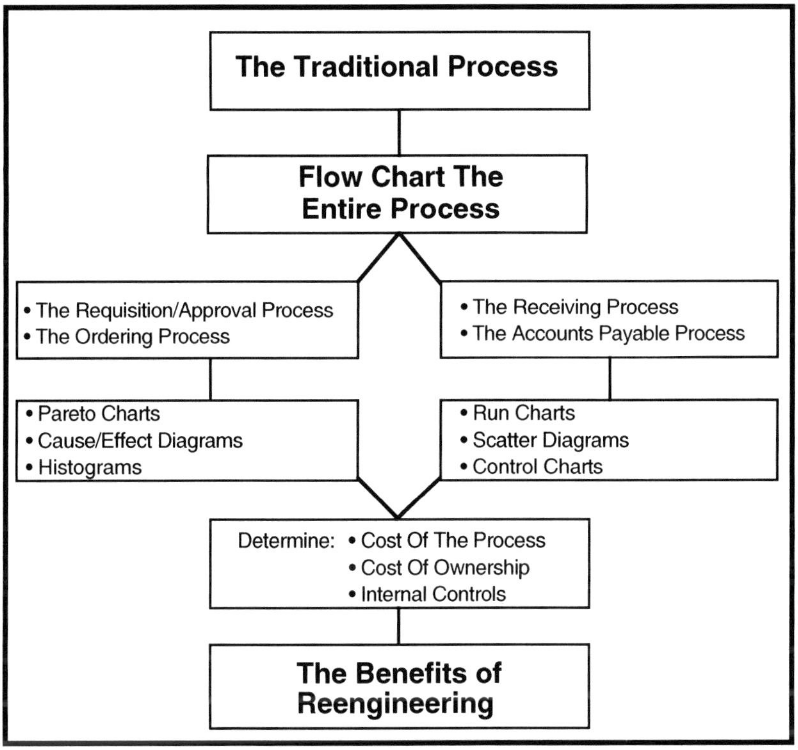

Figure 2.4

either had to be borrowed at an expense and/or funds that could have been invested in other more profitable internal projects and investments or in more lucrative external stocks or securities.

Insurance Costs. Most companies take out insurance on their assets. Any incremental increase of $100K worth of inventory represents an additional asset on which insurance premiums must be paid.

Property Taxes. As with insurance, property taxes are levied on the assessed value of a firm's assets: the greater the inventory value, the greater the asset value, and consequently the higher the tax bill.

Storage Costs. The warehouse where a company places its inventory is depreciated by a certain amount a year and charged to operations. Therefore, a direct relationship exists between the size of the inventory and the storage space required. Reducing the need for the inventory to be on hand will enable a company to downsize its warehouse operation and free up such valuable space to manufacturing where it can add value. The opportunity in the area of MRO inventory reduction is huge considering the fact that the average traditional company manages to turn its inventory just once a year versus world class companies that achieve 100-360 turns.

Obsolescence and Deterioration. In most companies a certain amount of stock becomes spoil, is damaged, is pilfered or eventually becomes obsolete. No matter how diligently inventory or materials managers guard against these situations, a certain amount of inventory shrinkage takes place. With new products being introduced at a faster pace than ever and the continuous changes within our companies, the probability of obsolescence has increased accordingly. Consequently, the larger the inventory, the greater the absolute loss from this source. Again, within traditional companies we have huge opportunities, as typically 35% of the inventory is dead!

These are all expense categories that can be directly assessed against inventories. In addition to these expenses, companies sponsor considerable amounts of indirect expenses in managing these inventories, in reorganizing their warehouses and stockrooms, and in controlling the level of inventory accuracy. Generally all these expenses, both direct and indirect, rise and fall with the inventory level. Maintaining inventory is expensive and should be treated with great care.

Reengineering Further Defined

Chapter Three

3.1 Why Change?

Where do we go from here? Most procurement professionals are so involved in the day-to-day operations that they don't always feel sufficiently integrated enough to bring about change, especially change that has a profound impact upon the entire organization.

Since we are looking for profound and radical change, we must be prepared to start from scratch. Years of Continuous Improvement have brought about greater efficiencies, increased respect and selective partnerships for many purchasing organizations. However, we have not done enough, and reengineering becomes a priority if your area of responsibility is still impacted by or participates in the following non-value-adding activities:

- Processing of manual requisitions

- Auctioning of purchases
- Supplier invoice errors are common
- Working with noncertified suppliers
- Plagued with poor inventory turnovers
- Suffering from extended lead times
- Too many multiple sources

All of these activities are symptoms of the traditional process. The time has come to recruit support from upper management for reengineering.

3.2 What is Reengineering? How to Change?

To be credible, however, a well thought-out plan must be developed that recognizes the principles of reengineering by reinventing the entire process. According to the authors of *Reengineering the Corporation,* Michael Hammer and James Champy, reengineering means "starting all over, starting from scratch."

Your proposal to reengineer the procurement process must espouse their "three Rs:"

RETHINKING: An entire new way of thinking will be required.

REDESIGNING: A new process designed from scratch.

REIMPLEMENTING: Fully implement as if there were no process before.

It is imperative that the process map includes the entire procurement process from the point of use though Accounts Payable - i.e. across all the traditionally functional areas.

3.3 What Reengineering Is Not

"Reengineering" has been used in vain to cover-up serious business mistakes and as an excuse for downsizing without much substance. Such failures are the result of either a lack of business integrity or a lack of know-how. However, reengineering is certainly not one of the following concepts:

- Rebuilding of obsolete information systems
- Restructuring and / or downsizing
- Bureaucracy buster
- Total Quality Management program

3.4 Prerequisites to a Successful Reengineering Campaign

In addition to being committed to the three Rs, your proposal, in order to be successful, must identify the team that will set the direction and recognize the following prerequisites:

Process Champion. There is no substitute for good leadership, for without it process redesign will not come about. Only a very few within most companies have the vision, desire and ability to bring about significant change. This leadership should preferably be provided by an experienced change champion. Since we are focusing on the procurement process, we need someone with unilateral authority over the entire process, preferably the General Manager, to be the project sponsor and project champion. Only with this kind of support of the ultimate process owners can the Director of Purchasing in conjunction with the controller effectively function as the project leader. Outside guidance by a reengineering expert or consultant can be helpful in getting such a project off the ground.

Project Leader. The project leader must be held accountable to make it happen and through leadership and example bring about the support required for universal change. Someone who has demonstrated these abilities in other major successful projects is a prerequisite. A high level of energy and focus on what needs to get done is of the utmost importance. The leader must be able to attract the best talent.

Total Top Management Support, Top-Down. Lip service will not do. Management must not only be convinced, it must visibly show its support through organizational restructuring and by empowering its employees. Buy-in must be secured through leadership and cross-functional teaming.

Performance Measures. As has been said before, only what gets measured gets done. Identify a select number of attainable goals, establish realistic benchmarks and predetermine how and when to measure progress and status.

Decentralized Decision Making. Good leadership will stimulate the empowerment process and enable the various process owners to make the necessary decisions within their own areas of competency and responsibility. It is important that once teams make a decision that they receive full support and not be second guessed by management.

Accountability. Obviously, the team will need to be held accountable for the development and implementation of the reengineered process. The process champion must stay in close contact with the team and hold them accountable.

What an incredible opportunity - to start with a fresh sheet - to redesign your own job and remove the walls and obstacles that have prevented you from being the best you can be. But before you plunge in too fast, be guided by the following tips:

3.5 Tips on Reengineering

Customer Focus. The process must become driven to add value to your external customers. Unless it adds value, your customer won't be willing to pay for it - at least for not much longer. Again the measure is external customers and not internal customers, since once the process has been reengineered all internal forces better be working together to satisfy the external customer. The TQM approach, which concentrates on functional excellence in an attempt to hand-off the best work possible to the next function within the process, strongly promoted satisfying the internal customer but that has proven to be counter productive at times since it often leads to empire building and undesired controls.

Integration. Stand alone functions and procedures are a thing of the past. Processes must become integrated and perform seamlessly from customer requirements through planning, procurement, manufacturing, sales and distribution. A reduction in cycle time is a must.

Strategic Thinking. The project must have a strong sense of purpose and give your company the edge over your competitor. How can strategic supplier alliances add value to your customers through innovation and cost control?

Clear Target. Don't lose sight of your objectives; reducing costs while improving your ability to service your customer must remain the target. Eliminate negative internal competition.

Work Through Cross-Functional Teams. Management by decree is not very effective and not very lasting. To bring about change, have those who are part of the process help reengineer the process.

Secure Buy-In. Communication is very important as "buy-in" from both the top and the bottom is required to make it happen.

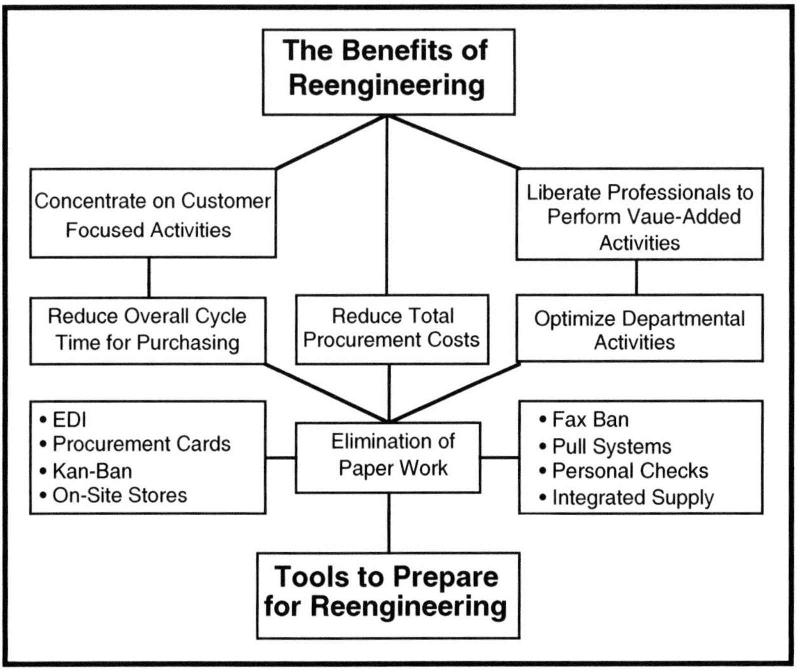

Figure 3.1

3.6 The Benefits of Reengineering the Procurement Process

To get results, you need to get to the core of your mission by rolling out a program that attacks current methods and procedures and develops a new process, as if you are starting anew. To make leap frog improvements you need to reroute transactions for replenishment directly into your suppliers. Furthermore, the process must challenge the entire Requisition to Accounts Payable process. This includes everything that transpires from the time a requisitioner determines a need through the final payment of an invoice.

At minimum this process must include:

- **Reduction of overall cycle time for Purchasing.**

Decentralize authorization & replenishment methods. It is important that all budget areas are not only responsible but also accountable for their own budget. Through redesign, Purchasing must provide the appropriate supplier agreements whereby the actual end user has greater control in authorizing the actual purchase or inventory replenishment.

Curtail approvals required. Through empowerment, the chain in approval command must be curtailed as all budget areas must be held accountable for their own spending.

Increase $ authorizations within areas of responsibility. By increasing authorization levels fewer approvals will be required, thus reducing the time it takes to make a purchase or replenish inventory.

Empower end users. End users, the consuming entity, should be in the best position to determine what and when materials or supplies are needed. By empowering the end users, the process will become more streamlined and curtailed.

Redesign the invoice reconciliation process. By moving the process of accumulating the necessary proof of authorization, proof of purchase, and the proof of receipt to either the end user or the supplier, a dramatic reduction in paperwork and time to reconcile such information will result.

Audits by exception. Rather than controlling a process into a finite degree both Purchasing and Accounting must develop audit and metric tools to ensure adherence and control.

- **Optimize Departmental Productivity**

  Increase departmental activities. Empower requisitioners and eliminate paperwork. A much greater level of autonomy by the user area will result in a faster, more direct and much more dynamic process.

  Purchasing must leverage high-volume purchases into programs. In order to enable the end users or consuming areas to have direct supplier contact, Purchasing must consolidate its supply base and implement programs whereby entire commodities are prenegotiated based on annual anticipated usage, along with predetermined release procedures.

  Receive directly into stocking areas or point of consumption. By having suppliers deliver directly into the area where the product is consumed, the traditional delays inside the receiving department and in the storeroom can be avoided resulting into dramatic process lead-time reductions. The verification of open orders and the development of a formal receiver are eliminated.

  Decentralize proof of receipts to suppliers. A substantial amount of bureaucracy may be avoided by placing the burden of proof of receipt upon the supplier instead of attempting to match and reconcile various documents from different internal control streams, three-way matching. This reversal in responsibility will substantially reduce the resources it requires to process invoices. Within Integrated Supply, the proof of receipt should clearly rest upon the shoulders of the supplier but should be monitored on an exception basis with the aid of a preapproved sampling plan.

Use procurement cards for nonrecurring supplies. For all nonstandard supplies or repair parts, obtained from nonstrategic suppliers, a procurement card should be used. This enables card holders to make direct purchases which must be charged directly to the appropriate cost centers. This should eliminate the need for petty cash as well. (See Chapter 5.8 on Procurement Cards.)

Eliminate need for receipt/P.O./invoice reconciliation. Integrators should be able to supply computer access, detailing all receipts against preestablished agreements. This should help reduce duplication and further eliminate the need for piles of paperwork. Suppliers should be requested to furnish detailed, signed packing lists, on a random basis for auditing purposes.

Convert to monthly consolidated invoices. Substantial amounts of paper work may be reduced by converting suppliers to monthly statement-type invoices along with the proof of delivery in the form of signed packing lists or computer generated data.

Elimination of supplier invoices. Those items that are system controlled and which are contracted on blanket orders or resupply orders for items with prices and conditions which are firm over an extended period of time. Payments for items received under these conditions can be created upon receipt. This eliminates the need for a formal supplier invoice, i.e. two-way matching.

- **Reduce Total Procurement Cost**

Curtail transaction costs for high-volume, low-value purchases. By going after the overall cycle time to purchase and by optimizing departmental activities substantial reductions in the cost of procurement can be made. These cost reductions include:

- Reduction in inventories.
- Reduction in purchasing staff.
- Reduction in Accounts Payable staff.
- Reduction or practical elimination of paper work.
- Improved efficiencies and reduced lead times.
- Reduction in cycle times.

Remove waste from all processes. If it doesn't add value (the end customer is not willing to pay for) it must add cost. Waste includes all those laborious transactions involved in procuring low-cost, high-volume supplies, unresponsive suppliers, outdated procurement policies and the Purchasing hierarchy itself.

- **Liberate Professionals to Perform Value-Added Activities**

  Strategically integrate suppliers at all levels. Suppliers are not the domain of Purchasing, but must be given the opportunity to vertically integrate with every appropriate area or department. By giving a supplier direct channels into the organization, new products and process improvements can be introduced and implemented at a faster pace and at a lower cost. Strategic MRO suppliers must have access to the following areas and departments:

  - **Purchasing:** Keep abreast of commercial and strategic direction
  - **Engineering:** Consult on future design specifications
  - **Maintenance:** Help reduce cost and resolve problems

- **Storeroom:** Help streamline processes, reduce inventory
- **Production:** Consult on safety issues, process improvement
- **Prod. Planning:** Communication of spike in demand

- **Concentrate on Customer-Focused Activities**

  Reengineering will bring about a cultural revolution which will enable us to become more customer- and process-focused. Through the new processes such as Supply Chain Management and Integrated Supply, Purchasing will now become responsible for:

  - technical innovation.
  - reduced internal cycle times.
  - reduced purchasing lead times.
  - improved productivity.
  - increased quality.
  - improved customer service.
  - cost control.

- **The Elimination of Paperwork**

  Paperwork elimination through new release methods. The implementation of Integrated Supply programs for reoccurring supplies and the deployment of procurement cards for nonrecurring supplies will substantially reduce operating costs.

Acknowledgments:

APICS Magazine – June 1995

NAPM Insights – June 1995

Reengineering the Corporation by Michael Hammer and James Champy

Chapter Four

Tools to Prepare For Reengineering

4.1 A Toolbox Full of Opportunities

Most companies are pursuing Continuous Improvement Processes within the framework of TQM. However, to be sustainable, these improvements must become interlinked into a fully reengineered process.

In order to fully prepare the environment for reengineering we need to eliminate unnecessary functions and aggressively optimize the core functions that will remain necessary within certain processes. The following "tools to prepare for reengineering" should be used as enablers to get the process going, to improve quality, to reduce costs and to get focused on the real core activities:

- **Lead Time Reduction**
- **Cycle Time Reduction**
- **Supplier Consolidations**
- **Empowerment**
- **TQM/CI**
- **Just-In-Time**

- **ABC Accounting**
- **Win/Win Negotiations**
- **Standardization**
- **Supplier Partnerships**
- **Supplier Certification**
- **Outsourcing**

4.2 Lead Time Reduction

Lead time reduction, along with cycle time reduction, has become one of the true business differentiators of the 1990s. Managing these two phenomena aggressively translates into speed and agility, which in turn allows successful organizations to reduce their inventories and costs while improving their quality and competitiveness. For the record, lead time represents the time that will elapse between the placement of an order and the receipt of the goods, materials or services. In many organizations this issue is very cloudy and confusing. Mismanagement of lead times or working with accumulative lead times can be self-destructive and make a business much more complex to manage. Accumulative lead time includes numerous activities that take place simultaneously that should be coordinated and consolidated. By studying a process and identifying the lead time for each step within the process much can be learned. Reengineering will aggressively attack these inefficiencies and design all accumulations out of the process. Purchasing is in a unique position to combat these problems by proactively slashing lead times and continuously demanding better performance and reduced lead times from its suppliers. Obviously this requires the buying organization to be willing to communicate critical information such as master schedules and production scheduling details and to share "best practices" concepts.

What Causes Long Lead Times?

Misconceptions. It's only natural to feel that the more time one has to complete a job, a task or an order, the better the chances are for a timely completion. But in fact with more products in the hopper and longer production runs, the greater the inefficiencies become. Long lead time problems are more of a symptom of the real cause: poor communications and extended set-ups.

Bureaucracy. Traditional processes are ineffective and cause additional and extended lead times because they require multiple approvals and are based on accumulative system lead times which makes the entire process cumbersome and uncompetitive.

Large lot sizes and high volumes. We have been cultured to think that ever-increasing volumes bring greater efficiencies and profits. We also assumed that we would have to work harder and faster to get jobs done in less time. However, two major paradigms shifts, which brought us the Total Quality Management approach in the 1980s and speed, or "time to market," in the 1990s, have drastically altered our views and beliefs.

Large inflexible supplier base. Having too many suppliers will prevent a company from standardizing and applying leverage in terms of both quality and cost upon its suppliers. Attempting to get control over thousands of suppliers is counterproductive and not manageable. However, working with targeted key partners within selected commodities can dramatically improve a company's ability to manage the process.

4.3 Cycle Time Reduction

The second pillar of the twin towers of breakthrough opportunities is cycle time reduction. Much of what happens in cycle time is in the area of white-collar, non-value-adding activities. Cycle time is the amount of time required to complete all the process necessary to fulfill an order.

Speed is of the essence in today's business environment and many companies have recognized that it may be the only market differentiator left between themselves and their competition. Driven primarily by consumer demand for services such as overnight package deliveries, video rentals, quick (20 minute) oil changes, instant replays - time compression or cycle time reduction has become a competitive weapon.

What Causes Long Cycle Times? Waiting in line in front of machinery or equipment is usually the cause for the long cycle times within manufacturing enterprises. Studies have shown that traditional processes have as much as a 20:1 ratio of wait time to "touch time," the actual time people or machines spend working on the item. Other causes for such delays might be poor communications, the batching of items within a process, serial versus parallel operations or an outdated factory layout causing extensive in-plant transit conditions.

Unfortunately, most processes are treated as stand alone functions within departments which causes much overlap and inefficiencies (functional silos). Also, the repetitive nature of many of the processes become self-serving, often causing a myopic attitude rather than a commitment to perform the cycles faster and more efficiently.

Some of the symptoms which might help identify a need for cycle time improvements:

- **Outdated, inefficient bureaucratic systems**
- **Numerous multipart forms**
- **Extensive approvals required**
- **Inventory imbalance**
- **Frequent engineering changes**
- **Constant expediting of schedules**

Most of these cycle times can be curtailed with little or no additional capital investment or human resources. Focusing on the process through process mapping will substantially improve most cycles. Suppliers, in particular those with a great deal of experience with Integrated Supply, should be pulled into the process evaluation early, since they have a great deal of experience in this area. As Bruce Stallings, Vice President of Operations for Plumbing & Industrial Supply in Evansville, Indiana states: "Do not leave us out. We make up 50% of the total process. We are the price, the packing list, the invoice and a potential source of errors and error solution."

Manufacturing organizations have some of the most recognizable cycle times:

Design & Product Development Cycle Time. Purchasing must be involved early to maximize supplier strategic positioning and performance.

Early Purchasing involvement can help reduce the R&D cycle time and impact the quality, cost, and availability of products.

Materials Cycle Time. This cycle starts as soon as the exact raw materials and/or components are identified and terminates when the products are delivered to the production line. The materials cycle time can be substantially curtailed through proactive purchasing and supplier management programs.

Requisition - Purchase Order Cycle Time. This often cumbersome process begins when a need is identified and ends when this need for materials or services is completed. This process covering the PR/PO cycle time can take anywhere from one day to several months depending on the complexity of the requirements and the caliber of the procurement department.

Inventory Cycle Time. As detailed under the Cost of Ownership segment in Chapter Two, inventories are expensive to maintain at an average cost of 2% per month of the original purchase price. The inventory cycle starts upon the receipt of the material and includes its storage, manufacturing time and finished goods periods.

Manufacturing Cycle Time. This cycle is interdependent with the inventory cycle as raw material gets transformed into finished goods during manufacturing. Improved systems such as MRP II and Just-In-Time have helped curtail the manufacturing cycle during the past two decades.

Other methods to reduce the manufacturing cycle time may include the following:

- Improved communications and forecasting
- Supplier scheduling
- Master scheduling
- Just-In-Time Manufacturing (JIT)
- Reduction in lot sizes and set-up times
- Decreased raw material lead times
- Reduced finished goods inventory levels

4. 4 Supplier Consolidation

The Total Quality Management Approach. Since the early 1980s, companies have become more aware of the benefits associated with supplier consolidations. Initially, the quality movement purely drove this process, in particular by the late Dr. Edward Deming and by the Statistical Process Control (SPC) movement that he promoted. By analyzing the data from the SPC process we learned that, while a multiple set of suppliers could meet the same product specifications, processing them intermittently, however, brought about downstream manufacturing variances. It appeared that even when two or more products met exacting specifications, each product had its own "fingerprint" or processing characteristics.

The Strategic Business Approach. Business and Procurement people alike quickly came to the realization that there was a great deal of value associated with leveraging volumes. Many examples of supplier consolidation have made the business headlines. Xerox reduced its supplier base from well over 3000 to approximately 500 suppliers. Even though this process has been in vogue for nearly 15 years, companies continue to downsize their supplier base. The initial focus in supplier consolidations emphasized the streamlining of raw materials and strategic materials. The second generation of consolidations was directed toward the MRO purchases. This highly undeveloped area continues to be the area of untapped opportunity through Integrated Supply and procurement card purchases. In December 1996, the Wall Street Journal, in a front-page bulletin, reported that: "nearly 75% of all companies anticipated substantial supplier consolidations in the upcoming year."

4.5 Activity Based Cost Accounting (ABC)

Activity Based Cost (ABC) and Activity Based Management Accounting (ABM) are exciting yet often misunderstood, new tools which enable us to better comprehend our true costs in procurement. The key ingredient in ABC & ABM is "activity" which calls us into action in measuring our true costs and in determining what causes these costs to occur in the first place. By identifying the cost drivers, we can determine whether or not these drivers are actually needed or add any value whatsoever to our existing process. Many of the activities the reengineering team will get into determine cost/value relationships in the daily tasks we perform. In order to exert control over these costs we must demand value and commitment from our strategic suppliers who can, provided they are given the opportunity, play a major role in reengineering the procurement process.

Cost reductions, and the elimination of costs related to activities that add no value to the product is one of the primary objectives in making our businesses more competitive. Traditionally, purchasing personnel are trained to focus on price and price alone, primarily because that's been the only measuring tool available to asses its financial impact and success. However, with the emergence of ABC Accounting, Purchasing now has potential access to accounting data and information that can provide valuable support in purchasing decisions. Procurement decisions may now be made on the basis of the cost of the individual transactions rather than just the purchased price alone. Activity Based Accounting will help identify cost reduction opportunities by exposing non-value-adding activities. As an example, many companies, with relatively few data points have come to the conclusion that Integrated Supply programs and procurement cards can substantially reduce in-house transaction costs for high-volume, low-value purchases. This example of an ABM application would allow a company to redirect its procurement resources to where it can impact the bottom line, rather than expending energy and resources on non-value-adding services and perceived controls. Activity Based Accounting should enable us to develop statistics, data points and justification to declare certain processes obsolete.

What Is the Definition of Activity Based Accounting? Activity Based Accounting is a method or tool that helps identify the activities and the costs associated with all activities as performed by your company. After identifying the costs, they are allocated - through the use of cost drivers - to the respective processes, products and services as performed.

How Much Does It Cost to Issue a Purchase Order? Activity Based Management enables us to dissect the variable costs associated with the issuance of purchase orders. This subject has become a hotly debated issue among many controllers, consultants, executives and procurement people alike. Inasmuch as we can calculate these variable costs, these sometimes highly exacerbated numbers become moot issues unless we tackle the process inefficiencies as demonstrated and highlighted by the ABM accounting process. This means we must disconnect certain functions, reengineer our processes and remove or reassign those people who do not add value.

How Do We Apply the Results of ABC/ABM? Once we have identified and defined the cost activities and their respective cost drivers, we need to take this data and put it to good use. By measuring the costs associated with all the activities within the procurement area, we have an opportunity to assess the value of each of these process steps. This in turn generates the following questions.

- What is the cost of issuing a purchase order?
- What is the value of clear and concise specifications?
- What is the cost of a supplier nonconformity?
- What is the cost of issuing RFQS?
- What is the supplier cost breakdown for goods and transportation?
- At which level of expense are negotiations desirable?
- What is the cost of a supplier missed delivery?
- What is the cost of dealing with too many suppliers?
- What is the value of certified versus approved suppliers?
- What is the cost of processing receipts?
- What is the cost of making general ledger entries and issuing checks?

The chart on the next page provides a comparison between the two different approaches to cost management.

The Activity Based Costing tool can also be used to measure how much it costs to deal with a certain supplier. For example, how much it costs to deal with a supplier who consistently ships late or who has occasional quality rejects. We can now calculate the amount of indirect costs associated with the purchase of capital equipment or to measure the cost of employing the entire supply chain. The data gathered in this evaluation process should be used in the launch of the reengineering project.

Traditional Cost Accounting	ABC Accounting
• Reactive data analysis	• Process-oriented
• Controlling	• Enabling
• Treats symptoms	• Root cause analysis
• Functional approach	• Extension of TQM efforts
• Tracks labor & machine rates	• Looks at total throughput
• Focus on allocation of indirect costs	• Assigns indirect cost based on cost drivers

Figure 4.1 Traditional vs. ABC Accounting

How Does ABC/ABM Work? How Are Activities Defined? The activities within the purchasing process are analyzed to determine the costs incurred by them, which are then allocated to the respective projects, materials and/or business units involved. The activities that are normally being tracked might include, but are not limited to, the following:

- Identifying and evaluating potential suppliers
- Request for Quotation projects
- Sourcing & negotiations
- Supplier visits/audits
- Awarding contracts
- Supplier certification
- Order placement and expediting/goods receipt
- Invoice processing and payment

Once the set of activities has been defined it will be necessary to identify the cost drivers of those activities. A cost driver is defined as the direct cause or the reason of the work, the specific thing or event that causes the work to be necessary. For example: order placement: "What causes a purchase order to be placed?" Requisitions would be the most logical answer in a traditional environment. With ABM, it is important to properly identify these drivers because it determines how costs will be allocated. The magnitude of the driver directly determines the extent of the work that will be created.

It is important to understand that costs are assigned at their "lowest identifiable level." Product-driven costs are assigned on a hierarchy of unit, batch, product line or facility level. Customer- driven costs are assigned to the order, customer, market or enterprise levels, while purchasing-driven costs are assigned to the requisitioner, manufacturing or enterprise levels. The success of an ABM management system is highly dependent upon the quality of the cost assignments.

4.6 Win/Win Negotiations

Traditional Negotiations. Negotiations in themselves are as old as mankind and some of the same practices and principles are still around. Especially when it comes to negotiations for price, we still tend to be narrowly focused and quickly lose sight of long-term implications such as the cost of acquisition, the cost of ownership, life-cycle costing, the cost of noncompliance, future relationships, and the cost of field failures and service.

The New Approach. As we reengineer the procurement process we must stay focused on the objectives of reducing total costs and an aggressive systems overhaul. The new process will require substantial supplier involvement and participation. In order to make this process work, supplier partnerships, which will require supplier integration at all levels, will be the cornerstone of our project. Consequently, we will need to negotiate on the basis of overall cost and value versus price. We should develop a long-term orientation and focus on strategic objectives such as quality, performance and reliability.

Common Drivers of Procurement Activities

Activity	Drivers
Purchase orders & change orders	Number of requisitions Number of storeroom releases Number of SKUs Number of P.O. changes
Supplier Management	Number of suppliers Clarity of specifications Supplier performance
Expediting	Number of scheduling changes Number of late deliveries
Supplier Management	Visit suppliers Receive suppliers Quality of suppliers Continuous improvement Supplier performance
Negotiate contracts	Time to prepare Time in negotiations Number of suppliers
Certifying suppliers	Supplier audits Establish & maintain system
Receiving	Number of receipts Number of deviations and rejects
Invoice payment	General ledger postings Number of checks issued Invoices without P.O. number

Figure 4.2

Win / Win or principled negotiations produce several benefits:

- An environment driven by and focused on the reengineering process.
- Both parties must meet their own legitimate interests.
- The resolution of conflicting interests.
- An agreement that is executable and durable.
- A focus on interests and not positions.

Winning: A Key to Long Term Success! We all learned early in life that winning is important - sibling rivalry starts at a very early age. Because of this culturization toward winning, many people, particularly those who have spent years in a purchasing environment, have difficulty understanding that Win / Win negotiations can produce two winners.

In today's competitive market we must make sure that we remain focused on the real competitor which means we need all the help we can get by forming the best team we can field. Since most manufacturing companies are merely a link in the supply chain between its suppliers and its customers these very same suppliers could be considered real strategic and potentially important team players. If we, in conjunction with our supplier, improve our process and lower our cost, we might be in a position to gain market share - additional business for all parties involved.

Win/Win Negotiation: Planning for Success. Win / Win relationships don't just happen overnight, they take time to evolve. In spite of the best intentions and best laid plans, many relationships fail to develop for a variety of reasons such as:

Market conditions	Ownership changes
Management changes	Lack of a champion
Inflated egos	Competitive threats

Changes in strategic direction	Changes in core competencies
Foreign competition	Currency fluctuations
Economic changes	Political changes

Other Resources. In addition to this material there are many library references available on Win/Win Negotiations such as: *Win-Win Negotiating* by Fred E. Jandt, *Persuasive Negotiating* by Herb Cohen and *Supplier Partnerships* by Timothy Van Mieghem.

4.7 Standardization

Just like mass production techniques which were predicated on the principle of uniformity and interchangeability, the entire procurement process can benefit substantially from standardization. Especially within the MRO environment a great deal of opportunities exist as our supplies and repair parts have become fragmented over the years as a result of a broad spectrum of suppliers. Supplier consolidation and control will enhance the standardization process and help reduce purchasing and manufacturing variations. The implementation of Integrated Supply will address this problem. As an example, a large automotive component plant traditionally purchased bearings from up to five different distributors. Even though the internal stores catalog specified a certain brand or equivalent, it turned out that in fact they hardly ever received the exact same product twice. Once Integrated Supply was implemented with a Single Source bearing supplier, certain unexplained equipment and processing variances disappeared and production became more consistent. It is imperative that purchasing drive the process of supplier and product standardization. The power of standardization can bring a substantial amount of leverage to an organization.

4.8 Just-In-Time

Even though we frequently talk about Just-In-Time (JIT) purchasing, most ironically such a process doesn't really exist, since it cannot be performed on its own merit without JIT manufacturing or JIT distribution. Therefore, as so many companies have learned the hard way, JIT is not an inventory reduction program. (Even though, if done properly, inventories will come down over time as a consequence of good practices.) Just-In-Time is all about the total elimination of waste. Whereas, maybe a decade ago we approached JIT from a product point of view within the context of TQM, today it has evolved into a process where all aspects of the Supply Chain come together in an agile environment. In the meantime, JIT has grown from buzzword status to a way-of-life in world-class companies. The entire concept of Integrated Supply is based on the JIT concept with strong emphasis on elimination of waste such as inventory, multiple suppliers, duplicate processes and components, and outdated systems.

4.9 Supplier Partnerships

Procurement professionals learned sometime ago that suppliers are no longer just the domain of purchasing. Rather, many companies are finding that once they shed their controversial buying methods that dramatic results that were once thought were unattainable can be achieved. **Supplier partnerships can bring about a strategic and competitive advantage by producing the following measurable and attainable results.**

- Understanding, reducing and controlling costs throughout the entire procurement process with cost savings through pure cost reduction, not necessarily just price reduction.
- Empowering and enabling the supplier to provide value-added services to your company's internal resources, as well as your end customers.

- Integrating processes where possible and most importantly in the procurement process itself by reducing waste and duplication.

The formation of a full partnership and strategic alliance can be measured by the presence of the following prerequisites:

- The supplier is positioned in a consultancy capacity and is viewed as a resource throughout the entire Supply Chain.
- Building trust is an essential ingredient and happens over time and will occur through the consistent exchange of information (financial statements, quality charts, cost analysis etc.) and through mutual goal setting and cross-company teaming.
- The entire agreement between the two companies is process mapped and fully documented as part of binding contract that includes pricing, service, measured goals and quality.
- The commitment by both parties must be long term (three to five years).
- The companies must integrate at all appropriate levels and include both top management and all relevant operations personnel.

4.10 Supplier Certification

When, driven by the TQM process, supplier consolidations and JIT became vogue in the early 1980s it was clear that supplier quality was of critical importance in our drive towards excellence. The need to certify our suppliers became critical as we moved from quality control to quality assurance and transferred the responsibility of quality onto our suppliers. The goals and expectations on supplier certification are driven by: quality, delivery and cost. The certification process typically consists of the following phases:

- Phase One = Develop historical profile & establish documentation
- Phase Two = Perform a supplier audit and process evaluation
- Phase Three = Finalization
- Phase Four = Qualification
- Phase Five = Audits & Maintenance

Supplier Certification is a component of the entire Supply Chain Management process and is therefore highly focused on suppliers of raw materials. Within Integrated Supply we do not tend to formally certify our suppliers, but many of the same techniques used to certify our suppliers are used as supplier developmental tools.

4.11 Outsourcing

During the past two decades American industry has completely rediscovered itself. By focusing aggressively on their core competencies, many companies have realized that numerous functions previously considered strategic were performed inefficiently and at high costs. Outsourcing has actually brought some companies from near collapse to prosperity. Chrysler is the biggest example of this when, after a government "bailout," it proceeded with closing numerous plants and aggressive outsourcing. This process, combined with a major commitment to the TQM process, played a major role in its comeback. We have come to the realization that companies can only be "world class" in a very few things. In the case of some automotive companies their core competencies appear to be limited to designing, assembling and marketing their products. The MRO buying process is well suited to be outsourced.

The New Process

Chapter Five

Now that we have established the benefits and maximized all TQM-driven functionalities we should be well prepared to transform these functions into interlinked activities. Now we are prepared to identify the new process.

5.1 The New Process Defined

Through process reengineering, procurement will transform into a "best practice" resource, which will transcend the flow of information between all the participants of the process. As referenced in Chapter One, the new process will, rather than the one size fits all, consist of four separate customer-driven processes depending on business strategy and application. These are the four primary processes:

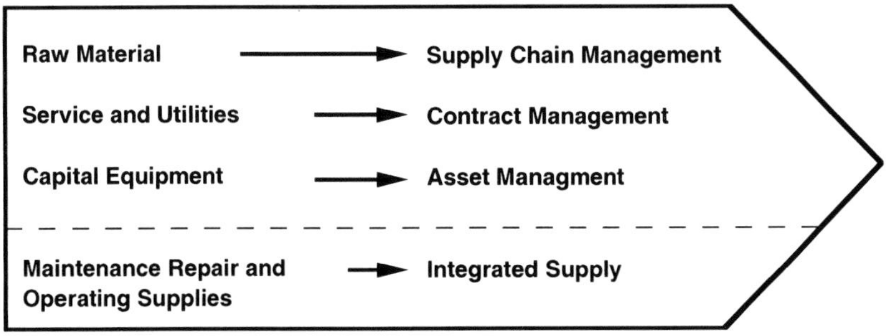

Figure 5.1

Each of these processes and the associated support processes will be covered in this chapter with the exception of Integrated Supply which will be covered in detail in Chapter Six.

5.2 Supply Chain Management

Supply Chain Management in its broadest context deals with the flow of material and information from the natural resource stage all the way through to the ultimate customer. Consequently, supply chains cover several enterprises such as raw material suppliers, companies who transform the material by adding value, finished goods suppliers, distributors and retailers. In order to optimize our business processes, we must make sure that all the resources within the supply chain share the gained benefits equitably. On a more local level, this means that a manufacturer will include both its suppliers and customers in the supply chain with the intent of minimizing constraints and addressing all major business objectives. These objectives almost always include issues such as:

- Inventory reduction at all levels.
- Reductions in lead time and cycle time.
- Development of EDI with suppliers and customers.
- Improvement in the order fulfillment process.
- Improved customer service and customer satisfaction.

By maximizing all the imperative operating variables, Supply Chain Management tends to have a profound impact on corporate earnings and shareholder value. All those companies that aspire to an integrated, world class, global order fulfillment process have embraced the Supply Chain Management philosophy.

Procurement's Role in Supply Chain Management. In order to facilitate a seamless raw material supply process a new culture must evolve, one of "Total Customer Focus and Satisfaction." Procurement must be proactive in planning its raw material requirements. This includes the involvement of:

- Active supplier partnerships / supplier certification.
- Aid to suppliers in the redesign of manufacturing processes (cell manufacturing).
- Reduction in cycle time and lead time.
- Forecasting in short-, mid- & long-term increments.
- Development of Electronic Commerce.
- Redefining the process.

To accomplish the above, Procurement must drive change and communicate the new objectives exceedingly well.

The Difference Between Supply Chain Management and Integrated Supply. Supply Chain Management focuses on optimizing the flow of products a manufacturer produces whereas; Integrated Supply optimizes the MRO supply process a company requires in producing these products. In Integrated Supply many of the same concepts and techniques as in Supply Chain Management are applied in that both the supplier and the customer (end user) become part of the same process.

5.3 Contract Management

Through Business Process Reengineering (BPR) Purchasing has been relieved from the day-to-day buying and replenishment process. This process revolution has resulted in the need for a higher level and more educated purchasing professional. Whereas, in the traditional process many high caliber plant and clerical people came up through the ranks, today's emerging purchasing professionals are more likely to be college educated and certified practitioners. As demonstrated in Figure 2.3, the new professional now spends up to 50% of his time managing contracts both within his own as well as within his suppliers' organizations. This is where Purchasing transcends (does not take ownership of) the flow of information between all the participants in the process. Purchasing plays this role as it provides the process link between users and suppliers.

Even though now that the purchasing professional is organizationally divorced from the buying (replenishment) process, sourcing in itself remains a strategic process. The matrix organization referred to in Chapter One places Purchasing on a cross-functional level with Marketing, Research & Development, Engineering, Production and Quality Assurance. The actual buying process should be performed at the plant or consumption level in a redesigned process that is void of paper and which facilitates direct supplier integration.

Types of Contracts or Agreements Involved. Which type of contract or agreement to use depends on the following: types of goods or services we intend to contract for, company size, industry type, level of supplier integration and $ value. Here are some options:

- **Formal contracts:** Raw materials, strategic components, capital equipment, health care, utilities, insurance, legal services, long distance
- **Partnership agreements:** Integrated Supply, outsourcing, early supplier development
- **Blanket orders:** Raw materials, strategic components, repair parts, facility & equipment maintenance, computer & communication services

- **Lease agreements:** Leases and rentals
- **Letters of intent:** Early supplier development, capital equipment

How to Use Partnership Agreements and Blanket Orders:

The Partnership Agreement can be used by itself or as an addendum to a blanket order. Such agreements should define all the steps the two parties have agreed to, including all obligations and responsibilities, as well as all the internal steps and procedures. It should also include a process map.

Partnership Agreements and blanket orders provide a unique opportunity for process improvement and standardization by detailing all these otherwise so loosely or noncontrolled "informal" arrangements for services such as: building maintenance, equipment and material handling, lawn care, janitorial and cleaning services, periodic inspections, snow removal, fire equipment maintenance, pest control and any other service for maintenance related services. Without up-front coordination and process control over these areas, the accounts payable area will be highly dysfunctional.

Product and service standardization of processes is of the utmost importance and a key success factor in controlling and managing the work load. In addition to raw material, components and factory supplies - many products and services can and should be standardized. A major bank in Philadelphia standardized its copier requirements for its corporate headquarters and more than 65 branch offices into one brand with a single supplier. The bank entered into a cost per copy program at $.0225 per copy which included equipment use, maintenance and all supplies except paper. This project alone allowed for the consolidation of nine copier brands, 18 suppliers and the elimination of literally thousands of documents consisting of requisitions, purchases orders, lease agreements, maintenance agreements, receiving reports and invoices. All of this has been replaced by one

Partnership Agreement and one monthly statement invoice which details: the equipment location, model and serial number, copies consumed, and the cost account and general ledger code for each unit.

Utilities. The acquisition and management of utilities is new and virgin territory for the procurement & materials management professional, in spite of the fact that the cost of energy amounts to as much as 15% of the total cost in heavy industries. Now that we are in the early stages of buying and managing utilities on an interstate basis, an entirely new opportunity awaits those who want to aggressively manage their costs. Commodities such as natural gas, electricity, water, and telephone are included in Utility Management.

Health Care and Insurance. During the past decade the cost of health care and associated insurance premiums has skyrocketed, with the total cost approaching 12% of our Gross Domestic Product (GDP). Now that most of the "low hanging fruit" has been picked and threatening suppliers has finally been recognized as unproductive, it is a natural evolution for purchasing professionals to become involved in this upscale commodity.

5.4 Asset Management

Due to its heavy focus on nonstrategic items such as MRO, Purchasing heretofore has pretty much abdicated the acquisition process of the companies' assets such as capital equipment, buildings and systems. Asset Procurement refers to the entire process of planning, organizing, and directing the acquisition and the disposal of assets. Asset Management, on the other hand, deals with the control, maintenance and security aspects of company assets. Both Asset Procurement and Asset Management has been highly decentralized up until this point as various entities, such as Engineering, Accounting and Facilities Management, all have had a piece of this. However, with the increased emphasis on Materials Management, serious consideration should be given to consolidating the accountability for the management of assets within this group. By taking a process approach toward the control and acquisition of assets, improvements in lead time, performance, standardization, supplier participation, accountability and total cost can be measured and be substantial.

5.5 Integrated Supply (See Chapter 6)

5.6 Support Processes

In order maximize our primary processes it will be necessary to have a good understanding of how various support processes can make significant contributions toward that end. The support processes shown below have been identified.

- Electronic Catalogs
- EDI
- Internet/Intranet
- Procurement Cards
- Maintenance Mgmt. Systems
- Monthly Billing
- Payments Without Invoices
- Electronic Three-Way Matching

(Electronic Catalogs, EDI, Internet/Intranet → Electronic Purchasing)

Figure 5.2 Support Processes

How these support processes can bolster the primary processes is covered in the remainder of this book.

5.7 Store & Maintenance Management Systems

Many corporations have combined their maintenance and storeroom functions into a streamlined integrated process over the past few years. This process is limited to the controlled items that are kept within the storeroom. The controlled items usually consist of repair or replacement parts, some of which may have been capitalized over the years. Unlike operating supplies, these items are often the critical components in keeping a highly reliable plant up and running. Additionally, these items are often on equipment Bill of Materials and are tied into a predictive maintenance management program. The release of these items from the storeroom often occurs as the result of a maintenance work-order. The mainframe or a PC-driven Stores & Maintenance Management System manages the inventory replenishment of the items into the storeroom. Upon reaching the minimum inventory level an automated requisition will be systems' generated. Upon approval by a storeroom attendant the system will auto generate and fax a release to the predetermined supplier of this product. Often a number of Integrated Supply partners such as: Industrial Supply, Electrical Supply, Bearings and potentially several others, provide both the Supplier Managed Inventories as well as numerous controlled items. Even though internal controls exist for certain items, suppliers can still participate as partners and replenish inventory up to the predetermined maximum level. However, such items should be bar-coded and be entered as a receipt into the system upon replenishment.

5.8 Procurement Cards

One of the hottest topics in the purchasing arena in the mid-1990s is the procurement card. Many companies have embraced the card as a "quick fix" for the paper work monster. Also, because of its potential to contribute to reengineering efforts, procurement cards are growing at a spectacular rate. Naturally, this conversion is being fueled by banks and major credit card issuers which are positioning for an early jump on market share for this very large, and, compared to consumer credit cards, very safe, and lucrative market.

Objectives of a Procurement Card Program:

- Streamline acquisition processes and reduce high-volume, low-value transactions.
- Reduce cycle time for acquisition of supply items.
- Empower employees. Make them responsible for their own small purchases.
- Have end users reconcile all receipts and procurement card billing.
- Monitoring of expenses at a macro level through summary reports.

Implementing a Procurement Card Program. In properly designed programs procurement cards get at the heart of the purchasing transaction problems in that they substantially reduce the cost per transaction, which ranges from $60 to $120 per purchase order in traditional organizations, to a mere $5 to $10 per procurement card transaction. The key ingredients are process redesign and automation. Usually, procurement cards are assigned to selected requisitioners who place their own orders directly with the authorized or preapproved supplier.

The Implementation Team. Once the top-down management support and commitment has been obtained a cross-functional implementation team should be formed which designs, develops, procedurizes, tests and implements the procurement card program. The team should have the following suggested representation:

Purchasing. This program is a very unique opportunity for Purchasing to bring about change and to shed its image as too control-oriented and non-value-adding. It is imperative that Purchasing looks upon this as an integral component of the reengineering strategy. Purchasing must aggressively support empowering the end user and not discourage them by placing too many restrictions on card use. One of the problems most companies experience is too much control over the Standard

Industrial Classification (SIC) codes in fear of abuse. This can lead to a blocking of retail establishments including Sears, which has a very valuable offering of MRO supplies. These types of controls have also caused many procurement card programs to remain stuck in the pilot program stage.

Accounting. With the potential of reducing transaction costs by as much as 90% and total paper work declining by nearly 65%, accounts payable departments are starting to realize that there is "life after month-end closing." The impact of paying in what amounts to as many as maybe 500 otherwise nuisance invoices in a matter of 15 minutes is very potent stuff indeed. Accounting must play a proactive role in developing these new processes, as without their total buy-in, all efforts will be doomed to failure. System design must address the posting to the General Ledger of purchases by cardholders so that this is done automatically upon payment of monthly statement.

Sales Tax. Expertise in this area is welcomed because of the thorny issue of state sales tax. Most states monitor and audit sales or consumption taxes very tightly. For that matter many companies are subjected to such audits annually - at considerable expense. At this time, only a number of card issuers have the ability to break out sales tax details on monthly procurement card statements which could lead to underpayment of taxes and subsequent penalties that sometimes runs into several hundred thousands of dollars for larger organizations.

Various options in dealing with the sales tax issue:

- Pay sales tax on all procurement card charges regardless of the nature of the purchase.
- Pay sales tax on all in-state purchases, assess each out of state purchase individually.
- Pay sales tax on all office purchases, assess each factory purchase individually.

(Please note that sales tax laws vary from state-to-state.)

Auditing. This process will need to be modified as well, since we no longer wish to audit the purchasing requisition and approval process as we have always known it to be. Auditing needs to support the new process by making sure spending limits and procedures are adhered to.

Several End Users. Getting the proper input from several future users of the program is important, especially since we need positive buy-in and a perspective that only they can provide. These chosen end users need to fully comprehend the current systems and its pitfalls so that they gain a real appreciation for the procurement card. It is also important that these end users actively participate in the pilot program and help sell its merits to their peers.

Additional Implementation Issues and Concerns. During the design, development, pilot testing and implementation stages the implementation team must be watchful for and take the following issues, opportunities and concerns under consideration:

- Resistance to change
- Align with a competent card provider
- Number of transactions involved
- Availability of mentors or other supporters
- Credibility of implementation team
- Assign site coordinator
- Development of an approved supplier list
- Determine hierarchy of control and reports desired
- Flow chart new process in detail

Placing safety parameters around the procurement card program:

- Spending authorizations are set at predetermined levels per transaction and per month.
- Purchasing & Accounting monitor the process while empowered end users control the individual trans-

action from purchase though receipt and monthly billing verification.

- Accountability of purchases rests with the card user and budget owner.
- System virtually eliminates formal paper transactions.
- Detailed spending reports are available by: individual, budget area, SIC code, and commodity.

Procurement Cards Are Ideally Suited for:

- Purchasing transactions limited to less than $1500
- Nonstrategic factory and office supplies
- Maintenance, Repair and Operating supplies
- Subscriptions, seminars and conferences
- R&D and laboratory supplies
- Transactions not covered by Integrated Supply, blanket orders, or Partnership Agreements
- Satellite offices or locations
- Elimination of petty cash
- Computer software

Program Administrator. After the implementation team dissolves, a program administrator will provide the coordination between the cardholders, Purchasing, Accounting and the card provider. The administrator will have the following tasks:

- Supply ongoing training and manage cardholder database.
- Track all complaints, internal and external.
- Coordinate validity of approved supplier list with Purchasing.
- Collect and distribute statistics on card usage and performance.

How to Keep Your Procurement Card Energized. Early on most cardholders are reluctant to use their new tool, primarily since it is so radically different than the traditional process, but above all because they feel their every action and purchase is being monitored, analyzed and critiqued. Furthermore, being in direct contact with external sources can be quite intimidating to some individuals.

How to Make the Card More Popular:

- Use ghost accounts.
- Use card with blanket orders as a "release and pay" tool.
- Set up cards with local vendors for charges on capital projects with predetermined charge codes.
- Issue a card account to a contractor for direct billing to avoid "cost plus" on material acquisition costs.

5.9 Monthly Statement Billing

The new process will require suppliers to invoice their customers on a monthly basis. In addition to a detailed monthly statement, the supplier will be required to submit a proof of delivery by customer location. This process works very well in particular with Integrated Supply as the supplier manages the entire replenishment cycle on behalf of the customer.

5.10 Three-Way Matching

Traditionally managed companies have an infrastructure in place that matches each and every purchase order, formal receiving report and supplier invoice. Entire careers have been built on this concept which some companies, in fear of auditing, took to extremes by requesting invoices be submitted in duplicate. Within Integrated Supply however, we place the burden of proof of delivery upon the supplier. This can be accomplished in a number of ways:

- Supplier submits signed packing slips as an attachment to monthly invoice statement.
- Accounts Payable clerk requests proof of delivery based on a sampling plan.
- Supplier provides electronic proof of delivery.

Within the past two years many progressive accounting departments have bought into the concept of reengineering this entire process because of the sheer volume of paper work involved in the traditional process. With the ever-increasing demand for faster month-end closings, processing thousands of non-value-adding, low-value invoices became a critical bottleneck.

5.11 Payments Without Invoices (Self-Billing)

When structured properly, every receipt of controlled items generates a transaction. Some companies, upon receipt of such items automatically initiate the payment process without the need to match the purchase order and the formal receiver with a supplier invoice. Within 30 days after the receipt, or whatever the negotiated terms might be, the actual payment would be finalized. This process known as two-way matching is a very effective tool in reengineering the receipt-through-payment cycle. Obviously, in order to minimize disputes, this puts the onus on the buyer to maintain a perfectly pure database. Invoice-less payments are becoming increasingly more popular in the automotive industry. Often, this is associated with a consignment program whereby the customer will generate payment upon usage or upon shipment of its finished product.

Integrated Supply

Chapter Six

6.1 Integrated Supply Defined

Far and away, the most significantly impacted area for reengineering be will the plant Maintenance, Repair and Operating (MRO) supplies. If approached and managed properly there is no single, more fertile ground for efficiency improvement and cost reduction opportunity than the MRO buying process. Often littered with outdated procedures, hundreds of suppliers, excessive amounts of paper and superficial controls, this is the area that requires major surgery.

Under Integrated Supply, companies will go out and exclusively purchase a certain commodity from a niche supplier or from an Integrator who can serve all aspects of the business. According to Fritz Krahl, Sourcing and Maintenance Stores Leader for General Electric Plastics in Mount Vernon, Indiana, "Integrated Supply provides for a great deal of supplier input and consultancy. In particular in areas such as OSHSA, ISO and safety issues, Integrated Suppliers provide highly valuable expertise which not only saves the company money, but also helps the company standardize its processes and products." Krahl goes on to say that, "Under ISO 1910.119 no changes in replacement parts of any safety-related or critical applications are permitted without formal engineering approval. Integrated Supply plays a critical role in providing the required infrastructure and policing of this process."

Integrated Supply is a long-term agreement with a single source and is designed to reduce the cost of acquiring and owning inventories of MRO supplies. Whereas, Systems Contracting started out as a way to reduce bureaucracy, Integrated Supply takes the concept a step further and "integrates" the distributor into every step of the of the procurement process. Under Integrated Supply, distributors are empowered to replenish stocks as needed, up to predetermined levels, without receiving an order or a notification. Integrated Supply is an agreement between customer and supplier to consolidate and minimize the buying, storage, delivery and payable processes while accelerating continuous improvement. Integrated Suppliers usually spend a lot of time on site and may even have an office on the customer's premises.

6.2 Is Your Company Ready for Integrated Supply?

In order to succeed with the implementation and management of Integrated Supply your company must look upon the chosen supplier as a true business partner – an extension of your company. This means that the supplier needs access to the same information available to the purchasing department. Key people within the organization must have the ability to see the total cost picture by looking at cost instead of price. In reality, when dealing with a major Integrated Supply agreement, which may include more than 5,000 items, just about any individual item could be bought "cheaper" elsewhere. Because of this daily price exposure, Integrated Supply agreements will fail without the necessary upper management vision and support. It is imperative that the proper education and training be provided to the user and requisitioner communities so that they understand the basics of ABC/ABM accounting and how true costs are measured and allocated. Also, management will have to facilitate the required cultural evolution.

Entering into Integrated Supply requires an organization to be empowered and requires a full commitment to both TQM and reengineering. Unfortunately, Purchasing, in most companies, does not possess the vision or leadership to drive a major change process such as Integrated Supply. Traditionally, Purchasing has blamed Finance and Accounting for its problems and has convinced itself that those departments would never buy into such radical changes. Therefore, Integrated Supply is usually "sold" to general or plant management, often over the objection of Purchasing. Companies that are committed to the process, however, must bring their purchasing departments on board.

Integrated Supply requires companies to enter into supplier partnerships in order to enable relationships to go beyond the traditional buyer/seller interface. Suppliers are no longer the domain of Purchasing, but in fact are a resource to the entire organization.

6.3 Types of Integrated Supply

Multiple Integrators. A system whereby various separate single source relationships are entered into, dictated by the size and complexity of the commodities. The average manufacturing company ideally enters into five to nine separate Integrated Supply agreements. The actual number of agreements depends on the size and complexity of the organization and the caliber of the potential partners. The reason many companies prefer Multiple Integrators is their desire to maintain certain supplier relationships and to preserve the supplier product expertise and technical core competencies that only these suppliers can provide. Under this concept, the customer almost always manages his or her own storerooms.

Total Integrators. A system whereby one company has been awarded the business of performing all MRO supply activities for an organization. As companies come to the realization that buying and managing their own MRO supplies is a distraction of their core competency, they begin to consider outsourcing this entire process. In spite of union resistance, many successful companies have moved ahead and recruited on-site suppliers. Several large mining and manufacturing companies have a number of different suppliers located on their properties. These suppliers will often make deliveries directly to the job site. The activities these integrators provide include all the steps in the process, such as planning, procuring, inventory management and distribution of all the goods.

Under the Total Integrator concept the supplier must have a very good network and infrastructure of suppliers and often will enter into consortiums or cooperatives to assure rapid availability of products and to prevent having to pay the added costs in dealing with second and third tier sources.

Total Integrators are in a unique position in that they can truly help the customer reengineer its MRO procurement process by proactively participating in Business Process Reengineering (BPR) teams. Generally a minimum business of $1.0MM per annum is required to attract a supplier into this on-site concept.

Advantages of Total Integration

- Requisitions submitted directly to the supplier
- Products delivered directly to end user (optional)
- No inventory obsolescence

- No excess or wasted inventory
- Elimination of bureaucracy
- Charges made directly to the appropriate cost center
- Improvement in cash-flow

6.4 The Objectives of Integrated Supply

- Migration of authority and transactions to the end users
- Elimination of paper work
- Reduction or elimination of inventory
- Supplier consolidation
- Improvement in material flow
- Reductions in overall total costs
- Unit cost reductions and price stability
- Product and process standardization

6.5 Which Commodities to Consider for Integrated Supply

Whereas, Supply Chain Management is well suited for strategic raw materials, Integrated Supply is designed for the MRO environment. This is primarily because Integrated Supply addresses the high-volume, low-value products. Choosing which commodities to consider for Integrated Supply is often driven by both internal objectives and the external environment. In particular, numerous high-profile industrial or mill supply houses have developed a strong culture and a proven process for Integrated Supply. These suppliers can help companies customize a process for their unique requirements as each agreement has special needs and requirements.

Commodities Well Suited for Integrated Supply:

- Industrial supplies
- Electrical supplies
- Plumbing supplies
- Bearings, belt & motors

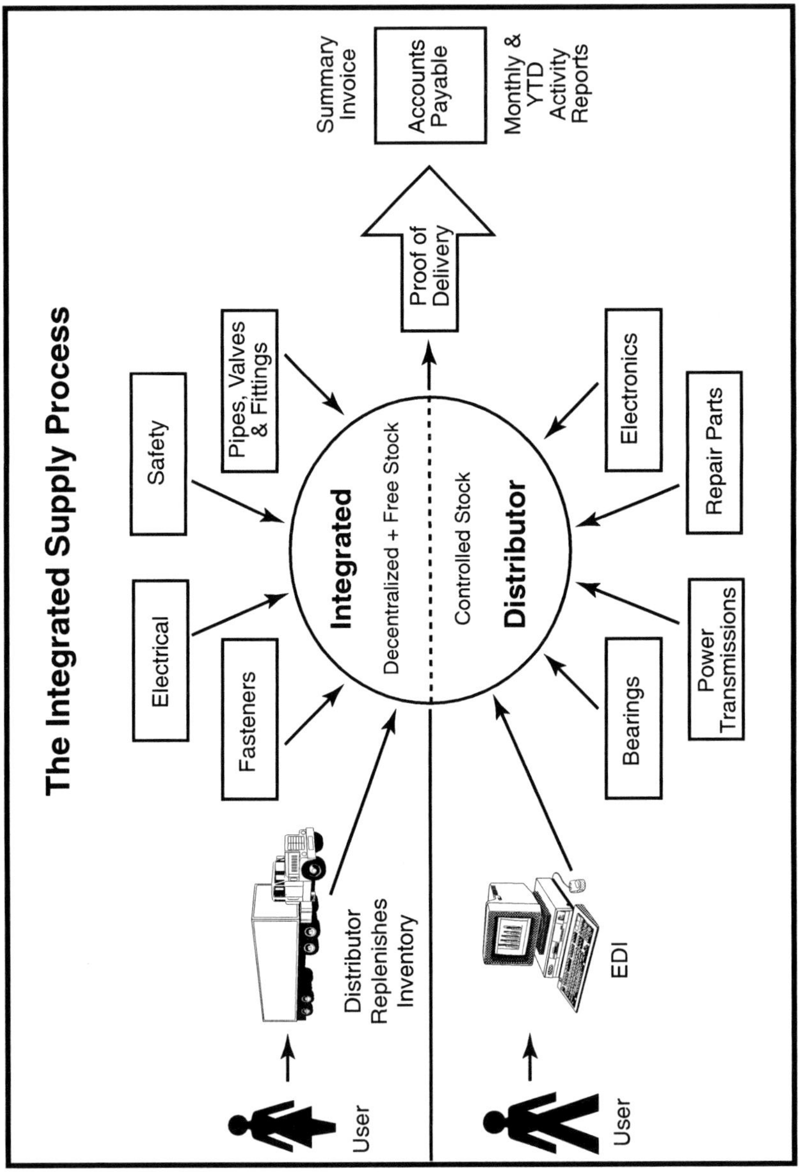
The Integrated Supply Process
User
Distributor Replenishes Inventory
User
EDI
Fasteners
Electrical
Safety
Pipes, Valves & Fittings
Bearings
Power Transmissions
Repair Parts
Electronics
Integrated
Decentralized + Free Stock
Controlled Stock
Distributor
Proof of Delivery
Summary Invoice
Accounts Payable
Monthly & YTD Activity Reports

Figure 6.1

- Fasteners and hardware
- Pipes, valves & fittings
- Fluids & chemicals
- Packaging supplies
- Janitorial & paper
- Power transmissions
- Safety supplies
- HVAC supplies
- Office supplies
- Computer supplies

6.6 How to Implement an Integrated Supply Program

To make Integrated Supply happen a lot of work needs to be done, especially initially because of the massive cultural change this new concept will bring about. At a minimum, the following steps will need to be taken:

- System analysis – benchmarking / best practices
- Establish cross-functional teams
- Decentralize supply items
- Determine which commodities to include
- Supplier evaluation and selection
- Supplier partnerships
- Negotiations
- Implementation
- Auditing

6.7 Systems Analysis

Benchmarking/Best Practices. Visiting with companies of like size and similar structure can give you a quick insight as to what the market is up to and what is out there in terms of "best practices." Also conducting internal surveys can help the change manager identify the needs of the employees. Recently, a reengineering team benchmarked itself with three other manufacturers and identified the following "best practices" for consideration:

- On-site stores
- Paperless invoicing
- Paperless purchasing
- Outsourcing

- Deliveries to end users
- Single Integrators
- Cost plus arrangements
- Procurement cards
- Meaningful metrics
- Decentralized inventories
- Bar coding
- Total Integrators
- Cross-functional teams
- Consigned stock
- Electronic commerce
- ABC accounting

System Analysis. In Chapter Two we covered the pitfalls of the traditional purchasing functions in detail. The flow charts as shown in Figure 2.1 clearly demonstrate how cumbersome these systems are. Since we also determined that the key focus in reengineering will be the area of MRO supplies, which again take up 80-90% of all transactions, the new process, in order to be considered reengineered, must bring about radical change – a rethinking of the way we do business.

Integrated Supply fits these prerequisites in that the reengineered process we seek to implement will remove Purchasing from the day-to-day execution process and eliminate the need for paper. The new system is one of employee empowerment, accountability and delegating of all activities down to the lowest possible authority. The change manager who is driving the reengineering effort must have an intimate knowledge of systems, process flows and best practices. After all, not only will the procurement function be impacted by radical change but also all the steps within that process. The storeroom in particular will require a massive overhaul and downsizing.

In designing new systems, the implementation team must differentiate early on between Supplier Managed Inventory and controlled items (those items which require internal structure).

Supplier Managed Inventory (SMI):

- Includes maintenance and consumable supply items
- Requires no internally controlled part numbers

- Tends to be of low value and is expensed upon payment
- Requires no formal receipt traceability
- Supplier delivers directly to point of use
- Supplier submits monthly/year-to-date reports by product and user area
- Audit by exception

Controlled Inventory Items. Even though portions of a commodity may be in a Supplier Managed Inventory Program, other products may require internal controls and the establishment of system part numbers for the following reasons:

- Repair items often are of substantial value and treated as an asset.
- Repair items are often included in equipment Bill of Materials so that future requirements can be projected for preventative maintenance programs.
- Replacement parts often may not be substituted for safety, ISO or efficiency reasons.
- Repair items often require extended lead times.

6.8 Establish Cross-Functional Integrated Supply Teams

Once a global systems review has been completed and a general agreement on reengineering has been committed to by top management, the Integrated Supply implementation team needs to be finalized and put to work. Since our primary goal is cleaning up the MRO mess, we need some serious representation from those functions that are impacted by the implementation of Integrated Supply. Quality and efficiency experts alike are very keen on teamwork. Cross functional teams or high-performance work teams have become common place in world class companies. Each person selected to participate on the Integrated Supply implementation team will represent a disci-

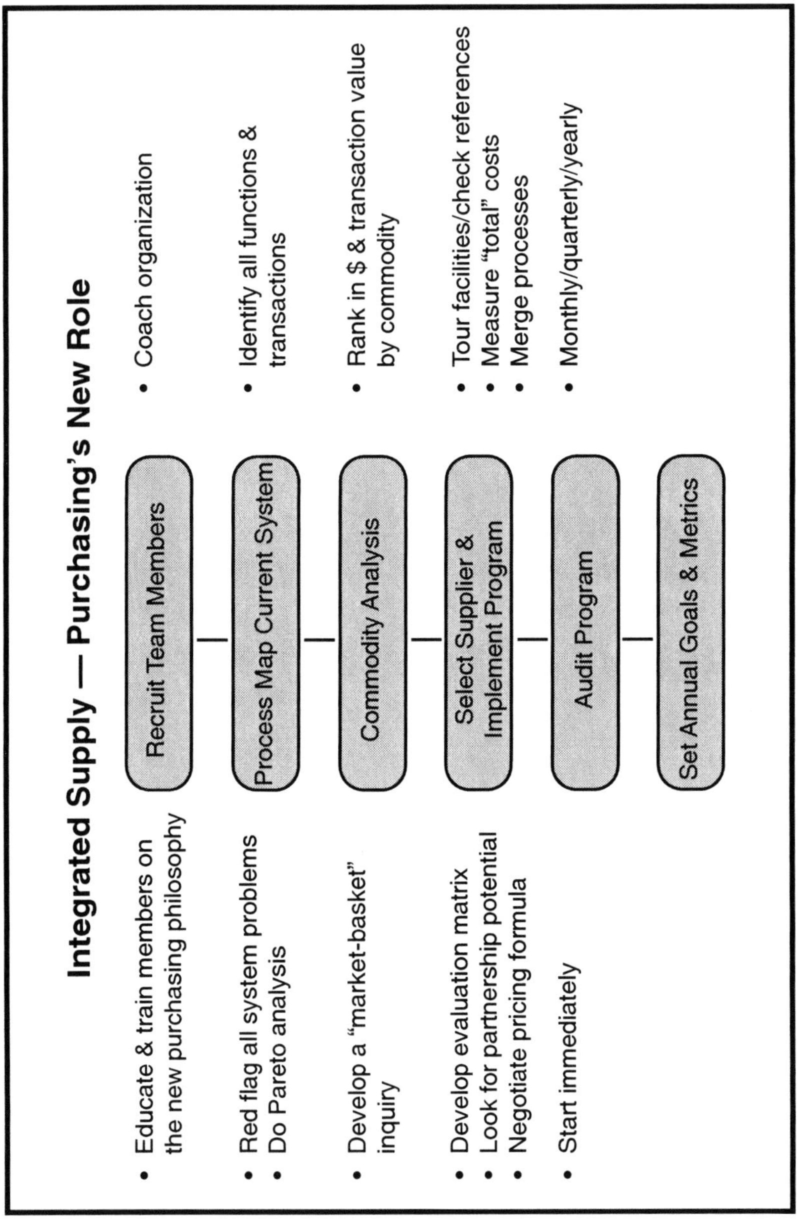
Integrated Supply — Purchasing's New Role
• Educate & train members on the new purchasing philosophy
Recruit Team Members
• Coach organization
• Red flag all system problems
• Do Pareto analysis
Process Map Current System
• Identify all functions & transactions
• Develop a "market-basket" inquiry
Commodity Analysis
• Rank in $ & transaction value by commodity
• Develop evaluation matrix
• Look for partnership potential
• Negotiate pricing formula
Select Supplier & Implement Program
• Tour facilities/check references
• Measure "total" costs
• Merge processes
• Start immediately
Audit Program
• Monthly/quarterly/yearly
Set Annual Goals & Metrics

Figure 6.2

pline and will add unique insights, perspectives and approaches to bring the team's total output beyond the sum of each individual's talents.

Cross-Functional Integrated Supply Implementation Team Membership

- Buyer
- Storeroom attendant
- Production worker
- Production supervisor
- Maintenance worker
- Accounts Payable

With the kind of representation shown above, along with a whole lot of additional coaching, you get more than just good synergy, you get the most important ingredient of all: **"buy-in."** After all, with the potential elimination of literally hundreds of suppliers, somebody's favorite supplier is going to be left out in the cold, or someone's favorite gadget or brand might get substituted. **An inordinate amount of emphasis is always placed on top management support, but in fact, buy-in at the plant level is every bit as important and often very much underestimated**. In particular, in old line and unionized manufacturing companies the maintenance group can, and often will, sabotage supplier consolidation programs. An electrical supply program might be doomed because of resistance toward a new product line such as fuses or control panels because some electricians will swear by a certain brand not available to the new supplier on a first tier basis.

Without Maintenance and Production support, these programs would be far more difficult to implement and difficult to sustain over the long term. Nevertheless, unreasonable resistance cannot be tolerated since the survival of the very organization is at stake. In as much as we want radical change – it takes time to change culture. By setting high standards and displaying excellent leadership, this process can and should be accomplished by and through the people that have to live with the end product.

Decentralization of Supply Items. At this stage of the game, now that the cross-functional teams have been formed, it is necessary to determine which supply items should be decentralized from the storeroom directly to the floor within a manufacturing cell. In the manufacturing environment we want our employees to have direct access to any supply item needed to keep the equipment running or to perform a quick set-up. Often these supply items are very basic and inexpensive. They usually include items such as clamps, pins, rivets, fasteners, brushes, silicon oil, tape and gaskets.

Which Commodities to Include. As previously stated, many commodities and even raw materials can be transformed into an Integrated Supply program. However, MRO supplies is the area that needs the most attention. Within that area, industrial supplies usually represents the largest commodity. Fortunately, just about every community has access to at least one industrial supply house that specializes in program and system selling. Better yet, these local or regional distributors are bound to be part of a national distributor network, a wholesale association, affiliation, alliance or a supply consortium. For details on alliances and consortiums see Chapter Seven.

6.9 Supplier Evaluation and Selection

Finding the ultimate supplier with excellent partnership potential is of critical importance to the success of Integrated Supply. In as much as we expect Integrated Supply partners to be competitive, we must make sure that such a measurement is based on a program in its entirety and not on a line item basis. After all, the system of getting low-ball prices for every item is the one we are trying to get away from – mainly because it is cost prohibitive and cumbersome.

Some companies, when going through the partner selection process, request each potential supplier to quote several thousand line items in detail. However, this is often a waste of valuable resources since 70% of all Integrated Supply inquiries are never awarded. Also, much of the data contained in inquiries, especially those submitted on disks with data downloaded from a mainframe computer, is often flawed, outdated and irrelevant. This process merely translates into one massive auction. A much preferred and more efficient method would be a spreadsheet of a representative sample of about 80-100 verified items representing a range in both value and volume.

Much to the frustration of some teams, some product lines as specified by either manufacturing or maintenance may not be substituted at any cost. Yet often these specific brands are not available from several of the most competent distributors. Such product lines are referred to as "franchise barriers." Allen-Bradley is a typical example: they have, to the dismay of many professional buyers, shown an incredible amount of distributor loyalty. The problem, according to many buyers, is that Allen Bradley does not necessarily surround itself with the most customer-focused and competent distributors. This discontent often results in second tier sourcing and the subsequent reduction in savings. Also, sometimes the first tier supplier is forced to "import" products from outside its own territory or state to satisfy customer needs.

At this point the team needs to develop supplier evaluation criteria and develop a list of the three to five most likely suppliers who could participate in the program. Once all the relative information has been compiled, the team must come to a consensus as to what is important to them and express this in a Supplier Evaluation Matrix. The selection criteria and the assigned values must be the same for each supplier within a commodity. The matrix will be used to score each supplier during the visit to the supplier facilities. (See Figure 6.3.)

In evaluating your suppliers you may use the following guidelines:

- **Customer Focus.** The supplier must be very focused on its current customers and be an empowered organization. If your company has an around the clock operation, you must have access to the supplier at any time during off-shifts, including weekends, if an emergency arises. Look for visible signs of customer focus in the order fulfillment and shipment preparation process. Ask penetrating questions about on-time delivery records. Does the supplier participate in point-of-use delivery programs? Make sure the supplier has a customer team concept in place as you do not wish to merely rely on a salesperson alone.
- **Inventory Depth and Breadth.** Does this supplier have a broad enough line to support your business? Does supplier have sufficient inventory to attain a continuously high service level?
- **Computer/Billing/Analytical Capabilities.** Make sure the supplier has the appropriate information technology to support your organization. It is important that the supplier is capable and willing to invoice monthly. Distributors have access to some dynamic software these days, much of which is capable of gathering sales data and statistics relative to your business. Basic monthly/year-to-date reports should be made available to customers.
- **Customer Dedicated Inventories.** Is the supplier willing, and does it have the internal controls, to carry customer-specific inventory?
- **Financial Strength.** Does this supplier have the financial strength to support your business not only today but in the foreseeable future as well? Consider the suppliers' market share. Can it sustain future growth, and can it survive competitive threats and economic downturns?

- **Ownership and Infrastructure.** Is the ownership active in the business? Is the business locally owned? Does it have other regional branches, and if so, do they provide backup inventories? Or is the distributor part of a national chain or network, and if so, can you negotiate an agreement for multiple facilities throughout the country?
- **Housekeeping and Safety Issues.** Research has shown that most successful companies maintain excellent housekeeping conditions. Warehouse locations should be well organized with a clearly defined space for every product.
- **Total Quality Management (TQM).** The supplier must be committed to this process throughout its entire organization. Make sure the supplier truly understands and lives this concept. Many companies use the TQM banner as a marketing tool while merely giving it lip service. Does the supplier have its process procedurized and flow-charted? Does it have a measurable continuous improvement process in place? Does the supplier actively participate in customer quality and process improvement teams? Has the supplier identified key business performance measures, and does it communicate these to employees and strategic customers?
- **Current Customer Contracts.** Does the supplier currently serve programs of a similar size or larger? Does the supplier have experience in maintaining other on-site stocking programs?
- **Customer References.** Whom else does the supplier provide similar services to and how do these customers rate the supplier's performance?

Other areas your team may wish to include in the rating are: staffing, shipping capabilities, communication tools, and community involvement.

INTEGRATED SUPPLY SUPPLIER EVALUATION FORM

SUPPLIER NAME: DATE:

SUPPLIER CONTACT: ANNUAL $ ACTIVITY:

SUPPLIER EVALUATION

DOES SUPPPLIER HAVE ...	VALUE	SCORE
commitment to customers?	15%	
inventory depth and breadth	15%	
computer/billing capabilities?	10%	
customer on-site inventory?	15%	
financial strength?	5%	
ownership and infrastructure?	15%	
housekeeping?	5%	
TQM development?	10%	
current customer contracts?	5%	
references?	5%	
TOTAL	**100%**	

Establish minimum performance criteria.

Figure 6.3

The Final Supplier Selection. Supplier facility visits normally take two to four hours depending on the supplier size and sophistication. (Sometimes follow-up visits are required.)

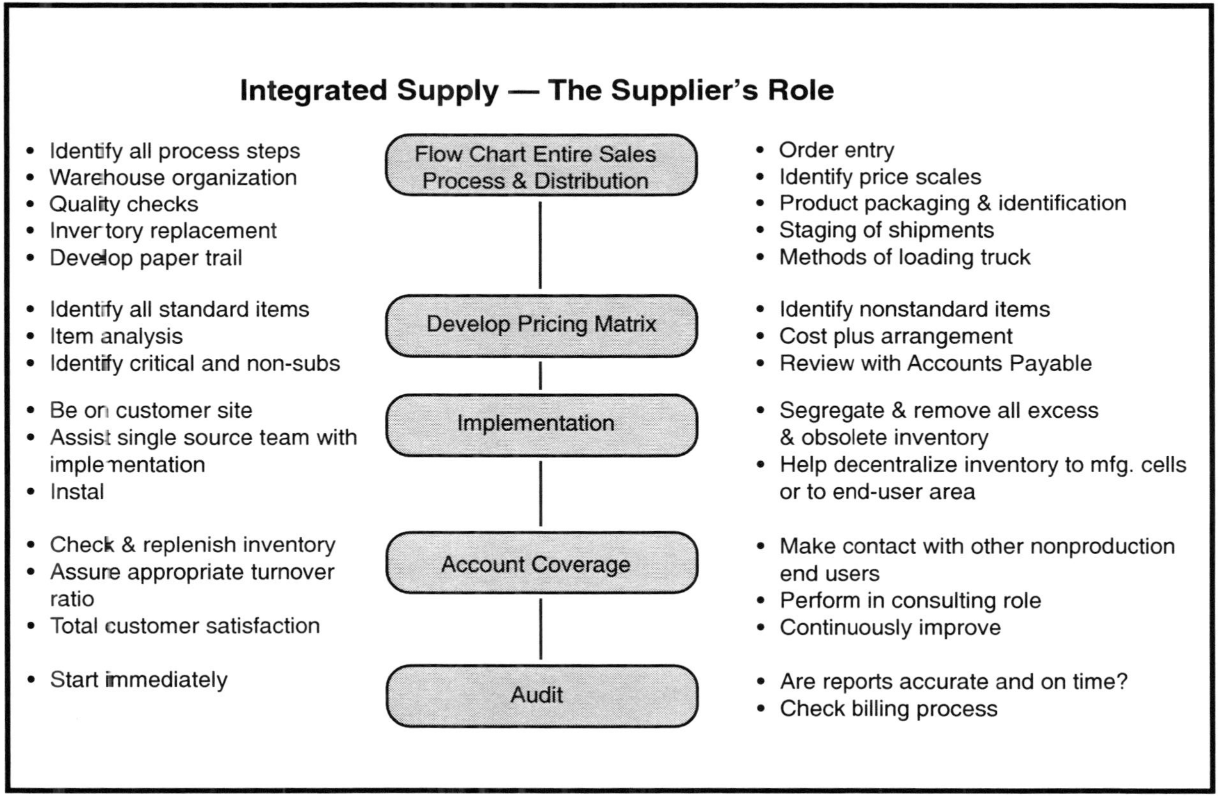
Integrated Supply — The Supplier's Role
Flow Chart Entire Sales Process & Distribution
• Identify all process steps
• Warehouse organization
• Quality checks
• Inventory replacement
• Develop paper trail
• Order entry
• Identify price scales
• Product packaging & identification
• Staging of shipments
• Methods of loading truck
Develop Pricing Matrix
• Identify all standard items
• Item analysis
• Identify critical and non-subs
• Identify nonstandard items
• Cost plus arrangement
• Review with Accounts Payable
Implementation
• Be on customer site
• Assist single source team with implementation
• Instal
• Segregate & remove all excess & obsolete inventory
• Help decentralize inventory to mfg. cells or to end-user area
Account Coverage
• Check & replenish inventory
• Assure appropriate turnover ratio
• Total customer satisfaction
• Make contact with other nonproduction end users
• Perform in consulting role
• Continuously improve
Audit
• Start immediately
• Are reports accurate and on time?
• Check billing process

Figure 6.4

Usually, the team leader opens the meeting with a brief statement of purpose. After this introduction, all team members join in and have an opportunity to ask all kinds of questions, or to listen intently, in order to help them form an opinion on the caliber of this potential Integrated Supply partner. It is important that the team stays in control of its own agenda and avoid a canned facility tour. Instead the team should be free to walk through the aisles and ask questions of warehouse and especially of delivery personnel.

Asking penetrating questions, especially in areas pertaining to service, delivery and the supplier paper trail, is of the utmost importance so that the team representatives get a comprehensive feel for this supplier prior to completing the Supplier Evaluation Matrix. Also, ask the warehouse personnel to show you the "returned goods" area, and how the Standard Operating Procedure deals with such deviations.

Template for supplier visit by self-directed, cross-functional shop team

Introduction: This team represents the XYZ Manufacturing Company, a locally operated metal fabrication plant of a major $5BM first tier automotive supplier.

- We are expanding our local business aggressively at a double-digit rate.
- We are an empowered organization that firmly believes in the TQM concept. We have given it the code name: Equal
- We are aggressively reengineering our plant's Purchasing process. We are focusing on reducing the in-house transactions from the demand created by the end user through the Accounts Payable process. We are seeking to select an Integrated Supply house that can manage all our electronic and electrical supplies.
- We already have entered into a number of important single source contracts with suppliers of other commodities such as industrial supplies, office supplies and hardware. We subscribe to the Multiple Integrator concept.

- The partnership we enter into will only be successful if it provides full supplier / customer integration at all the appropriate levels of the organization. Top management support within both companies is a must.
- We currently have 18 teams working on reengineering the procurement process.
- This particular team is working with five other single source teams in reorganizing the entire plant storeroom by decentralizing all production consumable items to the manufacturing floor, by removing all waste, by reducing the storeroom to 25% of its original size and by dedicating it to our maintenance group for emergency repair and replacement parts only.

Purpose of visit: The XYZ Manufacturing Company is seeking to implement a single source contract with a highly qualified electrical/ electronics supplier who subscribes to the same Total Quality Management philosophies that we abide by. We are here to assess your company's culture and your ability and desire to participate in such a program. Upon completion of our visit, this team will meet off-site to complete the *Single Source Supplier Evaluation Matrix*. (Show form.)

In exchange for single sourcing we have the following demands for the ultimate supplier of choice:

- A demonstrated commitment to Total Quality Management and Total Customer Satisfaction with a sustainable minimum on-time delivery performance of at least 99% within 24 hours on all standard items.
- The ability by the supplier to do a total assessment of customer requirements along with the establishment of a firm price catalog for all standard items and an agreement to supply all nonstandard items at invoice cost plus 15 percent.
- Be on customer site at least three times a week to check and replenish preestablished inventory within certain designated manufacturing cells and maintenance shop. (The number of visits will vary and must be suitable for each company.)
- Operate within a dynamic paperless process flow for all standard and nonstandard items.

- Have integrated computer systems that allow for monthly statement billing and provide for monthly/quarterly/annual reports on products and commodities supplied to each manufacturing cell. Have the ability to download all data via modem into customer LAN network in Excel.

6.10 Supplier Partnerships Within Integrated Supply

In Integrated Supply, partnerships with suppliers are of vital importance to keep the plant operating in a seamless matter while simultaneously controlling costs. Yet, these plant level partnerships are distinctly different from the typical corporate, market-driven, partnerships which center on the acquisition of raw materials. Whereas these corporate partnerships often include marketing and executive management, Integrated Supply agreements usually involve distributors and operate on a plant level. Integrated Supply tends to be highly focused on the end user. The real difference between these two different types of partnerships is that raw-material-type partnerships are strategic in nature with a limited amount of available suppliers, while the Integrated-Supply-type of partnerships are tactical in nature with plenty of potential participants. While vastly different in nature, implementing both types of partnerships is essential for our companies to keep the competitive edge.

Since Integrated Supply requires a different type of partnership, a different approach is therefore appropriate, namely in that these partnerships tend to be considerably more bottom-up driven than the typical raw material partnerships. For that reason we rely so heavily on teams made up of heretofore exclusively functionally-oriented individuals. For that reason it is imperative that shop, maintenance, accounting and storeroom personnel make up the majority of the team membership because it is these very same people who need to make the partnership work. The contribution by the other team members is more one of leadership and facilitating.

6.11 Negotiations Within Integrated Supply

The emphasis in negotiations for Integrated Supply agreements is geared toward performance, value and total cost containment. Experience has shown that those suppliers who score the highest in the *Single Source Supplier Evaluation Matrix* tend to be the low cost providers and therefore can afford to be price competitive as well. Thus, contrary to how we have been cultured and trained, we first select the most qualified, highest scoring supplier, and only then, after the selection process has been completed, do we negotiate the finite details and pricing. Throughout the entire process the supplier should be aware that you expect them to be competitive and cost conscious. According to Garry Beaudin, Vice President - Sales for C. N. Weber Industrial Products in Kitchener, Ontario, "Not all suppliers are capable of managing programs or systems because it requires investment and infrastructure." Mr. Beaudin estimates that nearly 80% of his company's industrial sales are program-related which demonstrates the major commitment his firm has made to Integrated Supply.

What to Include in Negotiations for Integrated Supply

- Finalize the scope of the product line or commodity
- Agreement and sign-off on the mutually developed process flow and process maps
- Agreement on what stock levels the supplier will maintain on customer site and in its own facilities
- Agreement on service performance measurements for standard and nonstandard items, including emergency deliveries
- Telephone or pager access to supplier during after hours and weekends
- Agreement on price method and structure. Could be cost plus or list price minus or depth of discount. Volume rebates might also be considered.
- Ability by supplier to develop Price Matrix on all standard items

6.12 Implementation

The proof of a major project like this is in the quality and the execution of the plans. Once we have decided upon the single source supplier of choice, and upon successful completion of negotiations, that supplier will play a key role in the entire implementation process. Because of all the work that has already been done thus far, such as the development of the process through planning and mapping, the analysis by the supplier of all the volumes and products, and the establishment of maximum inventory levels by line item, implementation should be well on its way.

Steps to be Completed for Full Implementation

- Supplier completes Pricing Matrix by supplier part number and by commodity code.
- Install *small* Kan-Ban containers or cabinets in user locations and / or maintenance department.
- Decentralize all manufacturing consumable supplies from the storeroom into user areas.
- Identify all supply items on containers or cabinets.
- Supplier bar-codes all containers and / or cabinets with part numbers.
- Accounts Payable department meets with core team and supplier personnel to review all process steps in detail.
- Introduce and communicate of new process to all end users.
- Cut-over of program.
- Schedule follow-up and audit session.

Other Implementation Issues. In the past few years many organizations have recognized the need to control the storeroom. A large percentage of these companies have even placed tool storerooms under very well disciplined inventory control systems and launched Electronic Data Interchange (EDI). This has been done to manage the number of physical daily transactions and in order to have access to more consumption data by user department. In itself this is quite a noble effort, but for many companies it is a very expensive, non-value-adding undertaking. Furthermore, the reality is that most computer transactions in a storeroom or shop environment almost always run from 2 to 24 hours behind while many small inconsequential transactions are never made until a stock-out occurs. Closely managing the inventories of nuts, bolts, rivets, pins, etc., the items with a per piece value of often less than $.10, could be extremely counterproductive and expensive.

Many companies currently implementing fully integrated computer systems, such as the highly regarded SAP program, are tempted, because of an ever increasing lust for data, traceability and accuracy, to assign a part number to every single supply item that enters the facility. The downside to such a desire for control is the inordinate amount of resources that are required to maintain data accuracy. (See Figure 6.6.) Therefore, it is extremely important that reengineering take place prior to, or at minimum, in conjunction with major systems implementations.

A close analysis of the process will help separate the factory Operating Supply Items from the true Maintenance and Repair parts. It is these Operating Supplies that are the nuisance items that make up 75% of the entire MRO process. This translates into 60% of the entire nonreengineered procurement cycle. It is imperative that these Operating Supplies be kept out of the mainframe planning and control loop and be placed into Supplier Managed Integrated Supply Programs.

Once those Operating Supply items have been reengineered out of the process, the real system design can begin. The factory Maintenance and Repair parts (the MR portion that is) can then easily be placed into SAP or any other operating system. Such systems will do an excellent job of tracking inventories,

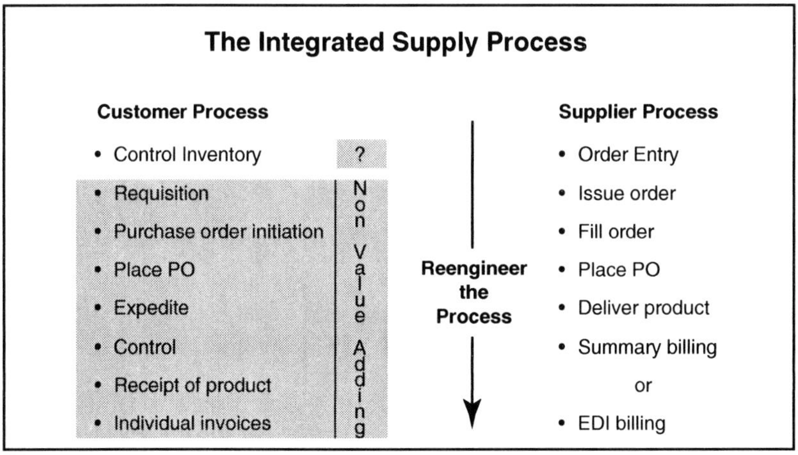

Figure 6.5

maintaining equipment Bill of Materials and in generating automated purchase order releases. Systems data accuracy and inventory accuracy become extremely important in a formal environment.

If and when properly designed and provided the proper infrastructure is in place, formal systems could play a value-adding link in the entire reengineering campaign. The actual design of the formal system will look different for most companies. It is also important that the organization be redesigned into a proper hierarchy and not into an ad-hoc environment. Many companies prefer to use more user-friendly Maintenance Management Systems and use them as a "bolt-on" in conjunction with their formal system.

6.13 Auditing the New Process

Once the implementation of Integrated Supply has been completed, an audit process needs to take over to ensure that all goals and objectives are met on a continuing basis.

INFRASTRUCTURE REQUIRED TO MAINTAIN MAJOR INTEGRATED SYSTEM

COMPUTER FILE	ESTABLISHED BY	PURPOSE
Item Master	R&D or Engineering	Basic Product Data Product Configuration
MRP-1 Screen	Materials Management	Material Group Procurement Type MRP Parameters Scheduling Data Min/Max Inventory Standard Lot Sizes
MRP-2 Screen	Materials Management	Availablity Checks ABC Indicators
MRP-2 Screen	Materials Management	Determine Conversion Factors Unit of Measures
Cost Screening	Accounting	Maintain Costing Data
Plant Stock	Materials Management	Warehousing & Storage Data

Figure 6.6

The following audit process is recommended:

Immediately. This part of the audit is especially important during the first several months since we are potentially eliminating hundreds of suppliers. A strong start and building upon this momentum are vital to the success of this major reengineering effort. Issues and performance criteria to check for:

- Are systems procedures and process maps working properly and being adhered to?
- Are all designated products as detailed in the Price Matrix purchased through the system and is the single source partner delivering product into stocking location within the agreed to time period?
- Are all requirements for nonstandard products with a value of less than $500 submitted to supplier via fax on a daily basis?

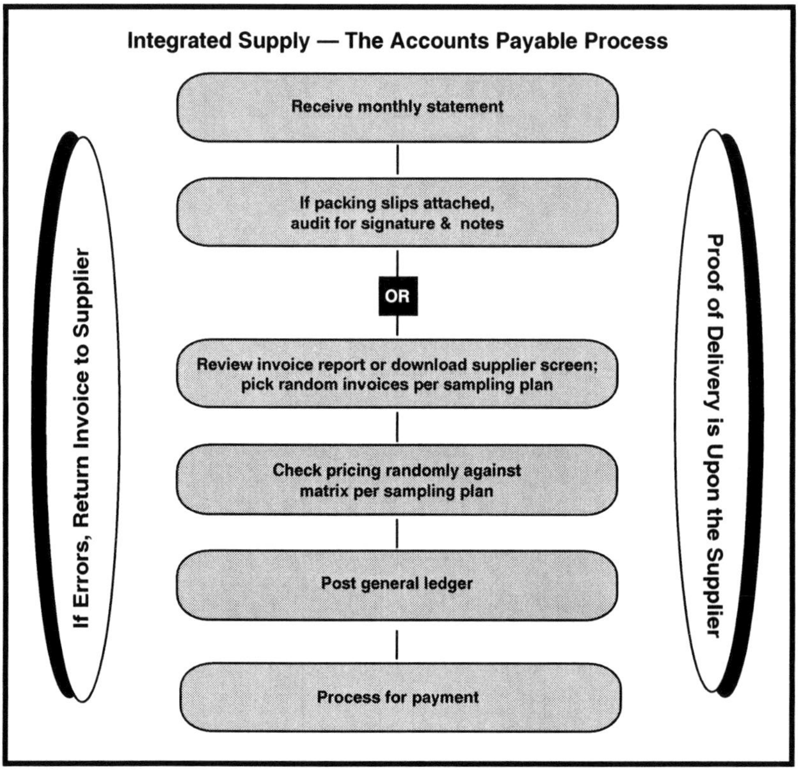

Figure 6.7

- Is supplier visible and on-site as needed?
- Is the supplier replenishing the inventory in a timely manner?
- Is the supplier maintaining a high level of accuracy?

Monthly. Once two or three months are under your belt, a new set of criteria is to be reviewed on a monthly basis.

- Analyze supplier monthly commodity report per layout requested.
- Meet with implementation team (first several months only).

- Confirm program adherence and comfort level.
- Meet informally with users, ask questions and solicit input.
- Are cost saving objectives being met?

Quarterly. Again, once up and running a small informal audit team made up of system users (including Accounts Payable) meets to monitor all Single Source Programs on a quarterly basis.

- Analyze supplier quarterly commodity report per layout requested.
- Does supplier properly restock up to maximum levels and keep place orderly?
- Make sure monthly statement billing program is working properly and that supplier provides signed proof of delivery upon request per sample plan.
- Is the monthly invoice paid on time?
- Are the inventory reduction targets being met?
- Is the product standardization process proceeding?
- Are the end users satisfied?

Annually. Once a year form a new audit team consisting of a plant or facility buyer, an accounts payable representative, a maintenance worker, a production worker and a plant supervisor. The objectives for this team are as follows:

- Analyze supplier annual commodity report per layout requested.
- Perform a systems diagnostic check to make sure process maps are up-to-date and that all user personnel understand and support the process.
- Make sure monthly statement billing functions properly.
- Develop supplier performance evaluation process. Meet with supplier and score supplier accordingly. (See sample Figure 6.8.)

- Check selectively what distributor pays manufacturer for its products. Are all savings and additional discounts passed on or shared? How about verifying invoices for nonstandard items?
- Develop new performance objectives and metrics for supplier for subsequent year.
- Coach suppliers and reassess process if supplier scores less than minimum.
- Determine if new suppliers need to brought into the process to replace nonperforming suppliers.

Another indicator as to how well the program is working is a verification check with systems and the end user.

INTEGRATED SUPPLY PERFORMANCE AUDIT FORM

SUPPLIER NAME: **DATE:**

SUPPLIER CONTACT: **ANNUAL $ ACTIVITY:**

SUPPLIER AUDIT

DOES SUPPPLIER ...	VALUE	SCORE
check inventory at regular intervals?	10%	
maintain 100% service level?	15%	
maintain inventory in an orderly and organized fashion?	10%	
follow procedures?	10%	
submit accurate billing with proof of delivery?	15%	
submit requested monthly, quarterly, and annual reports?	15%	
submit cost reduction suggestions?	15%	
introduce new products?	10%	
TOTAL	**100%**	

Establish minimum performance criteria.

Figure 6.8

Integrated Supply Performance Metrics

Business **Overall impact of program on the business**

Total annual sales volume with each partner
Total cost savings, direct and indirect
Reduction in total number of transaction
Value of consigned & owned MRO inventory
Indirect cost per transaction

Partners	**How have the partners benefited from the agreement?**
	Has the agreement resulted in a substantial increase in business?
	Is the partner given all the tools and access to succeed?
	Is the partner performing in a consultancy role?
End User	**Is the end user serviced better, quicker, and at a lower cost?**
	Total number of transaction
	% of service level
	Overall satisfaction rating – Has proper training been provided?
Operations	**Is the new system a better process?**
	% of systems versus MRO transactions
	% of items brought outside the Integrated Supply program
	% of problem invoice statements
	% of rush or emergency problems
	% of problem transactions
	Stock turnover ratio

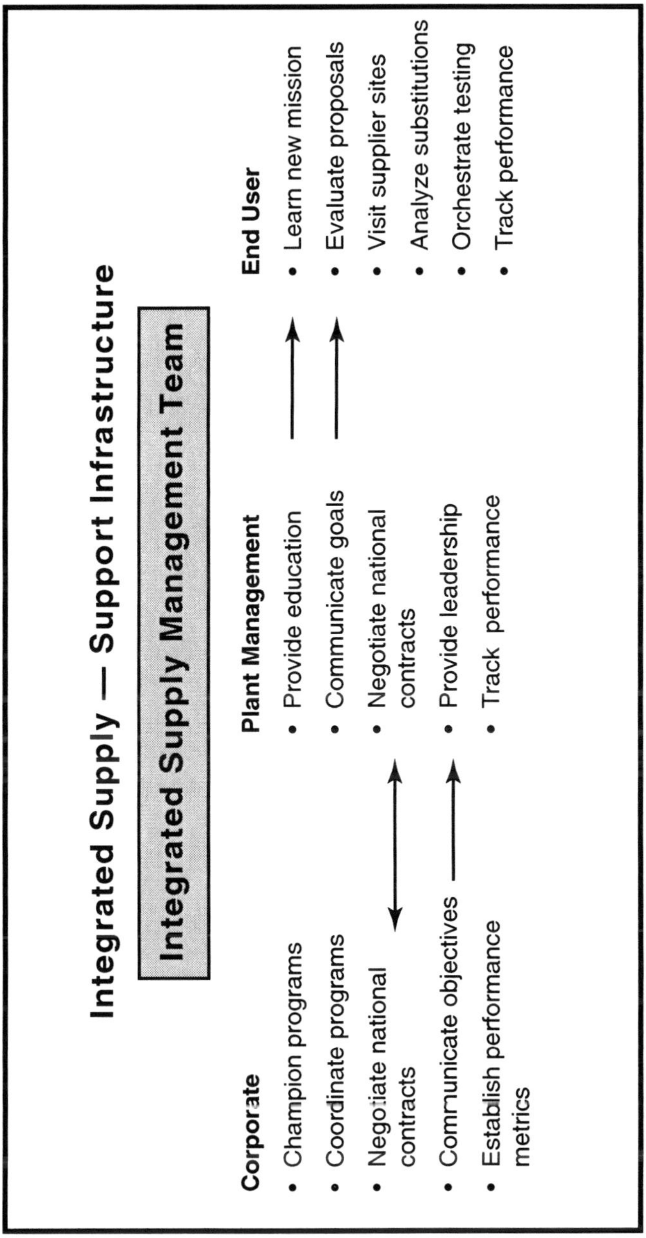
Integrated Supply — Support Infrastructure
Integrated Supply Management Team
Corporate
• Champion programs
• Coordinate programs
• Negotiate national contracts
• Communicate objectives
• Establish performance metrics
Plant Management
• Provide education
• Communicate goals
• Negotiate national contracts
• Provide leadership
• Track performance
End User
• Learn new mission
• Evaluate proposals
• Visit supplier sites
• Analyze substitutions
• Orchestrate testing
• Track performance

Figure 6.9

Upon completion of the Single Source Audit Process the ad-hoc audit team will be dismantled. Members may be called upon to participate in future audit teams for any given commodity.

The new process represents a dynamic, consolidated verifiable flow shown below.

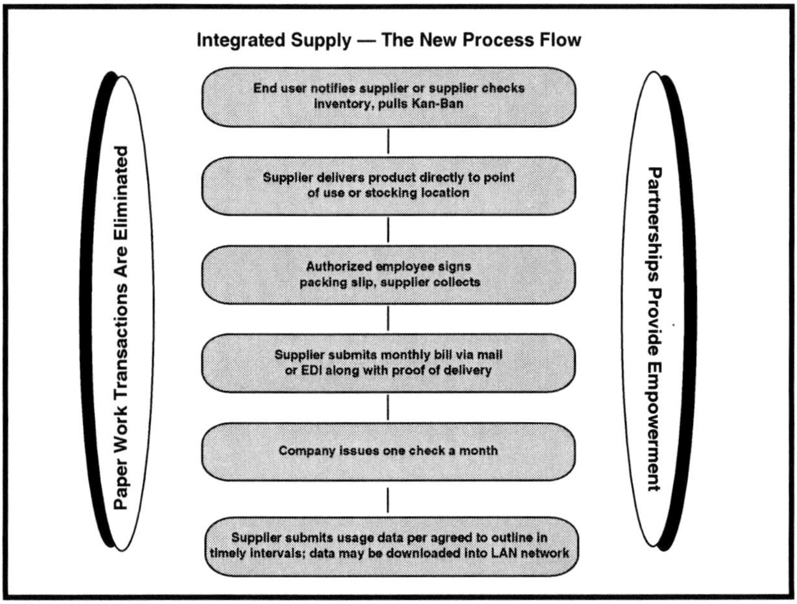

Figure 6.10

6.14 Cost Savings From Integrated Supply

Throughout this entire book, we have stressed the merits and necessity of measuring total cost versus price. But obviously total costs will not be positively impacted unless, in addition to aggressively changing the process, we substantially reduce or, better yet, eliminate inventories and dismantle the pre-reengineered organization.

Inventories, properly called the root of all evil, tend to hide our problems. An East Coast producer of components to the automotive aftermarket achieved a reduction in storeroom inventory of $2,000,000. This translated into a permanent cost reduction of $480,000 per year. Furthermore, the reengineered process should allow for the elimination of stock-outs and other heretofore uncontrolled issues.

Dismantling of the traditional organization must happen as the process is being reengineered. Reassigning personnel to other areas and / or responsibilities might be preferred, however unless that person specifically adds value in the new position, no financial benefits will be derived. Areas that will be impacted and where staff reductions related to this process must take place are in the following areas.

Purchasing. With a reengineered process and a substantial drop in work load, primarily in the amount of incoming requisitions and transactions, the elimination of daily spot buying or auctioning of MRO items and the sharp curtailment of visitors, the purchasing department must aggressively reorganize and downsize in order to reduce actual costs. The entire procurement world is full of exacerbated stories of how much it costs to issue a requisition / purchase order with numbers as high as $175 for such transactions. All of this is of total irrelevance until we cut the cord and make these costs go away ... permanently! Whereas, some talents might be transferable into value-adding activities, clerical duties and non-value-adding buying activities must disappear. Naturally, purchasing personnel should have opportunities to be placed in other areas of the company especially if the company has a strong educational culture and if the company is in a growth mode.

Storeroom. This area traditionally was perceived to be staffed with personnel who, through seniority, positioned themselves into early retirement jobs. This allegedly appeared to be the case in union shops where storerooms were often staffed with personnel who no longer could or desired to keep up with production. As the reengineered process calls for the elimination of most internal transactions, the storeroom staff should be trimmed and consist of production process experts.

Receiving. With the sharp reduction of suppliers and the delivery of many goods directly to the storeroom or end user, receiving activities are going to be very much restricted. Depending on the size of the company, the elimination of one or more jobs could be a reality.

Accounting. Much of what we are attempting to reengineer focuses sharply upon the clerical aspects of processing vast numbers of uncontrolled invoices. Once the process has been reengineered the work load in this area should be substantially reduced. In an average manufacturing company the amount of paper work and incoming invoices may be reduced by as much as 60%. Again, in order to truly reduce costs these jobs must be consolidated and excess personnel be reassigned or eliminated.

Net Impact of Cost Reductions. Based on the above detailed scenarios, the ABC Manufacturing Company, a $350MM supplier of components to the automotive aftermarket, was able to achieve, through the reengineering of the entire process, the following permanent cost reduction through inventory reductions and early retirements:

Inventory Reduction	$2.00MM @ 24% cost of ownership	=	$480,000
Purchasing	Elimination of two buyer positions	=	120,000
	Elimination of two clerical positions	=	60,000
Storeroom	Elimination of one supervisor position	=	40,000
	Elimination of two store clerks	=	60,000
Receiving	Elimination of one receiving clerk	=	25,000
Accounting	Elimination of three accounting clerks	=	90,000
	Elimination accts. payable supervisor	=	45,000
Total Savings		=	**$920,000**

Total Cost Reductions From Integrated Supply. In addition to the above detailed cost reductions (overhead), the ABC Manufacturing Company cleverly negotiated five single source Integrated Supply agreements and was able to reduce its product cost for the respective MRO commodities by approximately 12%. This resulted in additional savings of $180,000, and a grand total savings of an astounding $1,100,000.

Ironically, the process savings outperformed the actual product savings by a 5:1 ratio. Additional savings could be substantiated with the elimination of storage space and the cost of lost opportunity.

Integrated Supply Cost Reduction Opportunities Defined:

Procurement Costs	Product Costs
Reengineering of the process	Standardization
Inventory reductions	Leverage volumes into programs
Eliminate redundant positions	Reduction in variances
Curtail/eliminate storage space	Lower prices

6.15 Partnership Agreement for Integrated Supply

In the traditional purchasing environment, blanket orders had kind of a poor image and were battered around by controllers and administrative executives. This poor image was caused by the chronic lack of control that was exercised in such programs, as this tool was used to make open-ended, time-based, commitments and often provided for recurring deliveries of goods and services without checks or balances. This attempt of reducing paper work often resulted in inventory spikes or outages. If used within the proper context, blanket orders could be an excellent tool to manage supplier programs. The Partnership Agreement goes one step further however, in that it provides an entire process map for all the actions that need to be taken.

Purchasing's Role. In its attempt to migrate the daily controls and transactions to the end user, Purchasing's role becomes highly altered. The new role as it relates to the purchase of Maintenance, Repair and Operating supply items is one of leveraging entire commodities into single source programs. Purchasing will play much more of a macro role and is more interested in the overall benefits. Partnership Agreements should be updated at least annually.

Partnership Agreement Template:

Below is a template of a Partnership Agreement of the ABC Manufacturing Company for the purchase of industrial supplies with Apex, Inc. a local supply house. Apex is a single source supplier to ABC Manufacturing and maintains and manages all its industrial supply inventories. Also, this Partnership Agreement could be placed within a local area network (LAN) for easy access by all relevant personnel.

ABC Manufacturing Company, Inc.

Blanket Order # 96-112

Order issued to Apex, Inc.

This Partnership Agreement is issued to outline the procedures, process maps, pricing methods, and terms/conditions of the Integrated Supply agreement for industrial supplies program between the ABC Manufacturing Company and Apex, Inc. The account manager or his designate will visit each stocking location at least twice a week to monitor inventory and to meet with end users. All inventories to be replenished back up to the maximum allotted level; no minimums are to be maintained. Stocking items are broken down into two areas, Supplier Managed Inventory (SMI) items which require no items numbers or internal transactions and controlled items which do require an ABC Manufacturing item number and tracking number. Throughout the week the stores attendant may request additional standard and nonstandard items, via fax, on an as needed basis. No authorizations are required for any standard items up to any amount and for nonstandard items with a value of less than $500 per line item.

All shipments to replenish inventory to be on hand within 24 hours. All shipments must enter the building through the Maintenance Receiving Dock. Upon receipt of the product into the ABC Manufacturing Company the stores attendant will sign for the receipt of the packages and its contents. (Spot audits may be performed by the receiving department.) If an error is detected it will be handled immediately and all credits must be issued within the current billing cycle.

All pricing is per the signed Pricing Matrix, copies of which have been distributed to Accounts Payable, the storeroom attendant and the user departments. All those items which are nonstandard and not detailed in the Pricing Matrix will be billed at a price not exceeding the supplier's cost plus 15%, plus freight where applicable. The ABC Manufacturing Company reserves the right to audit supplier invoices to verify supplier's adherence to the pricing policy.

All part numbers are for reference purposes only, but will enable the supplier to provide detailed monthly, quarterly, and annual user reports by predetermined commodities, by department and by user location. These consumption reports will be provided either via e-mail or on a PC disk in Microsoft Windows 95 Excel format for downloading into the ABC Manufacturing's Local Area Network (LAN). ABC Manufacturing personnel may use the data at will to generate internal statistics, monitor usage and consumption trends by user area. All nonstandard or special items exceeding the value of $500 per line item must be covered by a separate authorization by the appropriate supervisor or by an electronic requisition/purchase order. All pricing under this agreement is firm through December 31, 19xx.

Invoicing will occur on a once per month basis for all items supplied under this agreement. Monthly invoice must consist of a statement detailing all packing slip numbers and the corresponding dollar amounts. No other details are required, however on a random basis, per an agreed to sampling plan, the accounts payable department will request the supplier to submit actual signed packing slips for auditing purposes.

Order Expiration Date: December 31, 19xx

Taxable Items: Those items deemed taxable have been predetermined based on its internal use application. A detailed spreadsheet, of those items considered taxable, has been developed and has been incorporated into the Pricing Matrix as designated with an (*). In the event an item is used in both taxable and nontaxable applications, sales taxes will be applicable as directed on the spreadsheet.

ABC Mfg. Internal Charge Codes:

Free-Bin items	=	GL 3225 CC 033
Standard items	=	GL 2225 CC 802
Nonstandard items	=	per release details

Performance Standards: A 100% service level must be maintained for all Supplier Managed Inventory (SMI) items and controlled items. Stock-outs, in the event they do occur, must be replenished within one hour. Nonstandard items must be filled within 24 hours and special items, those that the distributor does not and is not expected to stock, must be filled at a performance service level of no less than 98% within quoted lead-times. During off-shift hours and on weekends, the supplier must be on call in the event an emergency arises.

Storeroom: Aaron Lampton Tel. # 812-555-9999

Payment Terms: All supplier monthly statement invoices are subject to 2%-10, net-30 days.

Miscellaneous Issues: The supplier team led by the Account Manager will, at no further charges, assist ABC Manufacturing in consulting on safety, OSHA, ISO and processing issues on a day-to-day basis.

Purchasing Contact: MRO buyer Linda Corbett Tel. # 812-555-9988

Safety Conditions: While on-site, the employees of Apex, Inc. Company will obey all safety regulations including the wearing of hard hats, ear plugs, safety shoes and safety glasses in the so designated areas.

Liability Insurance: Apex, Inc. will supply the ABC Manufacturing Company with a certificate of proof of insurance naming ABC Manufacturing as the certificate holder. Minimum coverage $250,000.

Audits: An audit team consisting of five individuals including one representative from Purchasing and Accounts Payable and three end users from Production/Maintenance will meet quarterly and annually with the supplier team to discuss ongoing issues, monitor performance and establish goals and objectives.

6.16 Reorganizing for Change

It is very obvious that if we wish to accomplish and implement the kind of changes and programs implementations we have discussed in this chapter, we will have to reorganize accordingly. As we are elevating the procurement function from a transaction based function into a strategic new process, radical changes will be required throughout the company. The lack of follow through on reorganization and / or reassignment of personnel is the single biggest reason for the failure of reengineering campaigns.

Distribution

Chapter Seven

7.1 Distributors Versus Manufacturers

The value a distributor, wholesaler, jobber or mill supply house brings to the market can be quite substantial. Integrated Supply would be impossible for manufacturers to execute because it is beyond the realm of their core competency. Distributors, on the other hand, have, or at least should have, top-notch service as their primary objective. Early in the Industrial Age manufacturers sold almost exclusively "direct" to the end user. However, slowly but surely a power or positioning shift from the manufacturer to the distributor has taken place. The choice, if available, in dealing with either, is one of buying channels rather than one of proximity. In making this channel decision the question becomes, "What value does the distributor add to the process?"

Value-Adding Function of Distributors Over Manufacturers:

- Small lot distribution, lowest cost route
- Superior stocking and shipping capabilities
- Multiple product lines, numerous manufacturers, aggregation opportunities
- Enables buyers to consolidate suppliers
- Service is a core competency
- Merging of processes with customer
- Structured to supply emergency deliveries
- Ability to deliver directly to end user
- Ability to manage customer stock
- Access to network of affiliations or consortiums
- Ability to bill monthly by consumption area
- Lower per unit selling expense
- Responsiveness, flexibility and accessibility
- Customized services

Advantages in Buying Directly From Manufacturers

- Potentially lower prices for high volumes (truck load – who wants it?)
- Manufacturing is the core competency of supplier
- Greater product expertise (if you can get the access)
- Potential of optimizing manufacturing processes

Based on the overwhelming demands of small lot supply, the distributor obviously plays a key role in the procurement and supply process for many companies. Small volume supply items are almost exclusively purchased from distributors, as manufacturers do not have the infrastructure to manage such business niches directly. Some manufacturers, however, have developed their own distributor network in order to assure access to end customers and to reap additional revenues. These supplier-owned distributors, such as General Electric Supply, usually carry additional product lines to complement their own. Another major MRO supplier, Parker Hannifin, has created a franchise network, called iPower, which it sells to distributors. The franchise holders have access to and share the same software enabling them to place orders for their own and complementary products.

7.2 Local Versus National Distributors

In some companies the great debate centers on what is better: a locally owned and operated distributor versus a national distributor. Both have their pros and cons.

Local Distributors. In each and every community, there is at least one locally or regionally owned and operated distributor of industrial, electrical or mechanical type of supplies. The level of these distributors' quality and sophistication depends on the size of the market and the national affiliation(s) to which these suppliers belong. Independent distributors are finally flexing their muscles through a network of affiliations and consortiums, as they are now aggressively pursuing national clients which will be serviced through local affiliates closest to the location of the actual consuming plant. Fully integrated computer networks and consolidated monthly billing are now offered by some of the larger and more powerful affiliations.

Advantages of Local Versus National Distributors

- Broader and deeper local inventories
- Greater product expertise
- Local sales and technical support
- Strong personal relationships
- More resources on hand to service the customer
- Provides a feeling of buying within the community

- Local senior management and/or ownership
- Continuity, lower turn-over
- More flexible, innovative and entrepreneurial
- Lower overhead structure/low cost provider
- Around the clock emergency support

National Distributors. In spite of the fact that we have seen a great deal of decentralization take place in industry within the past two decades, a much greater level of emphasis has been placed on coordination between plants. This is chiefly the result of much improved information technology, better communication, and a need to get additional costs out of the business. The recognition and discovery of so many non-value-adding steps within manufacturing plants have generated a great deal of interest in Integrated Supply. Also within the past several years, major national distributors, distributor affiliations and consortiums of distributors have keenly marketed the need for program and systems buying. National distributors have strategically marketed their concepts to the executives of multi-plant organizations. This has resulted in large corporate contracts for these national distributors who can provide the necessary infrastructure and technical competency to make it happen at all the respective plants.

National distributors tend to carry leaner inventories per location but rely on overnight restocking and distribution efforts to satisfy their customers within 24 hours. Some distributors, such as Bearings Services, have a distribution network in place whereby orders placed into the system by 5.00 p.m. will be delivered to the individual branch prior to 6.00 a.m. Each region within their organization has a shuttle service or an extended "milk-route" that performs this stocking or resupply function. All successful national distributors have major regional distribution centers in place which are used as a hub to resupply their branches or to transfer stock between locations. The advantage is that a high service level, such as 24-hour delivery performance, can be maintained with a relatively low but rapidly turning inventory.

National or regional distributors of industrial supplies in particular have enjoyed a tremendous growth during the past decade. Cambar, also known as Cameron and Barkley, is one such organization, which supplies a full line of industrial, electrical and mechanical supplies to major, multi-site manufacturing organizations throughout the country. According to Randy Mints, Business Manager for Cambar in Louisville, Kentucky, his company markets its services to customers based on the following three core competencies his organization possesses:

- **Provide strong distribution Materials Management skills.** Integrate within customer and assume the entire role of the single source MRO supplier. Cambar seeks to capture at least 90% of that entire commodity with the only exclusions usually being office supplies, capital or OEM purchases, computer hardware/software supplies and contract services.
- **Provide strong technical competency.**
  - Be a problem solver: participate in production and maintenance planning sessions
  - Meet with process engineers and be exposed to all other departments
  - Conduct periodic review meetings with end users
  - Be a technical consultant and resource: be involved early with new equipment purchases to advise on component part standardization
  - Play the role of a troubleshooter: help resolve issues as they arise
  - Conduct safety seminars on customer site
  - Provide cost reduction programs and seminars

- **Leverage the entire purchase**. Stress total cost reduction and total cost performance. Provide full Electronic Data Interchange capabilities, implement bar coding down to line item level detail, manage or comanage MRO inventory on site and/or deliver goods directly to the end user. Take over as much as possible of the entire MRO supply process so that the customer may stay focused on its own core competencies. Continuously measure and communicate cost and service level performance.

7.3 Distributor Affiliations, Alliances & Consortiums

Although still somewhat in its infancy, within the past several years a new phenomena has arisen wherein a large number of independent distributors have formed alliances or have entered into a consortium of suppliers in order to offer even greater supplier consolidation opportunities to buyers eager and under constant pressure to further reduce their MRO supplier base. Manufacturing companies have done an excellent job in rationalizing the supply chain with suppliers of raw materials over the past decade or so. Now the push is on to get rid of this last great bastion of purchasing power: multiple suppliers and an expensive bureaucratic hierarchy in place to procure basic MRO supplies. Consequently, in the mid-1990s a very aggressive growth in new MRO marketing concepts has been launched with major consortiums and affiliations posturing themselves for large, lucrative contracts with major, multi-plant, manufacturing companies.

Affiliations. Affiliations are high profile marketing and buying groups that link together a large number of independent distributors. The purpose of affiliations is to enable their members to share resources and marketing expertise to compete with national distributors or wholesale chains. Without such a network or an affiliation, locally owned and operated distributors would be unable to compete for multi-plant contracts with locations outside their own geographical area. Until just a few years ago, local distributors were rapidly losing ground to national distributors - even in cases where they were doing an excellent job with long established customers.

Whereas, in the past, independent distributors were left out in the cold when plant purchasing coordinated its buying leverage with sister plants, today affiliations have enabled these same distributors to compete quite successfully with national distributors. Recently a major international pharmaceutical company coordinated the purchases of all its industrial and electrical supplies into an Integrated Supply Agreement for all 15 of its U.S.-based plants. After an intensive market search, a long-term agreement was awarded to an affiliation whose member independent distributors, located within communities near the respective plants, will execute the agreement.

With a desire by so many companies to downsize their own direct buying facilities and migrate most of the mundane transactions to their carefully chosen supplier partners, a much greater deal of sophistication and infrastructure by such suppliers has become mandatory. This is primarily driven by these large, multi-plant, multi-location national account type customers. Therefore, alliances and affiliations are considered a defensive as well as an offensive strategy, but very much a customer-driven issue. Probably the best example of a group of distributors that has been formed is that of Affiliated Distributors. A-D was founded in 1981 and is the largest distributor network in North America. This affiliation is comprised of over 250 local, independent distributors of electrical, industrial and PVF products whose collective sales approach $10 billion in North America. A-D is the only group of distributors that is nationwide in scope and offers customers both Integrated Supply programs and national single commodity type contracts.

According to Chris Hartman, Vice President and General Manager for Affiliated Distributors in Wayne, Pennsylvania, independent distributors join his affiliation for the following reasons:

- **The national account and Integrated Supply capabilities**. The national network affiliation gives independent distributors an opportunity not only to survive but also to prosper. Through direct affiliations the distributor is capable of supplying up to 70% of the MRO market while with the aid of product allies, distributors can indirectly supply 100% of the MRO requirements. Furthermore, and maybe the most important aspect, the affiliation provides the legal basis for multi-distributor contracts. Without the benefits of such an organized affiliation, independent distributors would infringe upon the law if they were to team-up and offer like pricing to multi-plant locations. It would be considered price fixing.
- **Financial incentive both in buying and selling.** Due to the significant amount of purchasing power, affiliate members can take advantage of deeper manufacturers' discounts and consequently be very competitive. From a selling point of view, the affiliation can provide support in coordinating presentations, proposals, contracts, reporting, etc.
- **Cooperative marketing programs.** The average distributor is too small to hire a dedicated marketing manager and launch elaborate marketing campaigns. This is where the affiliation comes into play as it directs cooperative marketing programs and approach major multi-plant buyers as a cohesive unit.
- **Low membership dues.** Since the affiliation doesn't take direct ownership of any merchandise themselves but merely commits on behalf of its members, it is able to make large volume commitments at low

prices and with attractive payment terms. Consequently, this structure and the economies of scale allow for relatively low membership fees.

Quality and selectivity are of prime importance to the major affiliations, as they do not wish to be diluted by volume and territorial disputes. Again, according to Chris Hartman, these are some of the corporate characteristics his company looks for in potential new members:

- Solid local market share / financial stability
- Respectability and integrity
- Integrated Supply experience
- Full product line in area of specialization
- Value-adding capabilities
- Documented quality process
- Statistical performance benchmarks
- Experience with EDI and Bar Coding technologies
- Continuity

Supplier and Customer Consortiums

Supplier Consortiums. One such an alliance, International Supply Consortium (ISC), brings together already powerful organizations such as Bearings, Inc., Cambar, and McJunkin. The geographically well positioned firm W. W. Grainger has formed a powerful consortium with the likes of Kennametal, Motion Industries, Fastenal Company, Ferguson and others.

These ventures transform each of these suppliers into broader suppliers of MRO technologies, as compared to the more narrow focus of there own product lines. By combining their efforts they collectively may be supplying as much as 90% of all the MRO purchase transactions performed by a typical manufacturing company.

When buying from any of these suppliers belonging to a consortium, a customer will be able to place a single order, receive combined deliveries and just one consolidated invoice for all products from any of these participating partners. Information Technology plays a major role as software and networking ensures a seamless flow of transactions between the buyer and the consortium members. By placing orders on-line with any of these suppliers, an Integrated Supply catalog representing all the participating suppliers will enable the requisitioners or buyers to consolidate orders against discount prices as if the product were supplied by just one distributor. Again, because of the network capabilities, the key supplier will coordinate, obtain delivery of the goods from the consortium partners and deliver the product to the customer as one order followed up by one invoice.

In addition to the consortiums initiated by the major industrial supply houses, consortiums sometimes are formed by a small group of distributors who as a group can survive supplier consolidations but who as purely independent distributors would be unable to stay alive in consolidations at companies such as Ford Motor Company which is fully committed to reduce its supplier base from 50,000 to 5,000 suppliers. The small alliances, designed to protect market share, are sometimes referred to as "regional alliances" representing mixed product disciplines.

Thus in fact, these various distributors become suppliers to one another by basically pooling their resources. Consequently, independent distributors are almost forced to join an affiliation or a consortium in order to participate in large, competitive accounts. Buyers must be cautious however, that in their zealousness of consolidating suppliers they don't compromise high performance standards, quality and a loss of product application capability. Taking such drastic steps can seriously undermine the necessary reengineering focus.

Customer Consortiums. Customer cooperatives have been in existence for many years. However, most of these co-ops could be found in health care, retailing and agriculture – but not much within the manufacturing industry. However, in order to improve pricing, numerous industrial companies have teamed-up within the past few years in order to take advantage of their collective purchasing clout. The commodities these companies have focused on are industrial, electrical and janitorial supplies, paper goods and bearings. Unfortunately, many of these customer-initiated consortiums tend to focus too much on price. However, those companies that combine consortium buying with Integrated Supply will be able to generate meaningful savings.

7.4 The Optimum Number of Suppliers

With so much emphasis on process efficiencies and paper work elimination it is tempting to consider the one stop shopping approach offered by the Total Integrator as discussed in Chapter Six. To aid in the assessment of what is best for your company, consider the "Integrated Supply Supplier Reduction Model" (Figure 7.1).

The Integrated Supply Supplier Reduction Model is based on the concept that when a customer is looking at transaction costs involved in MRO purchases, transaction costs actually reduce with the number of suppliers. There are fewer relationships to manage, fewer transactions that take place, consolidated invoicing, fewer purchase transmittals, etc. So, if one were only looking at transaction costs, one would come to the conclusion that perhaps a single supplier (Total Integrator) would be the best option all the way around, including cost.

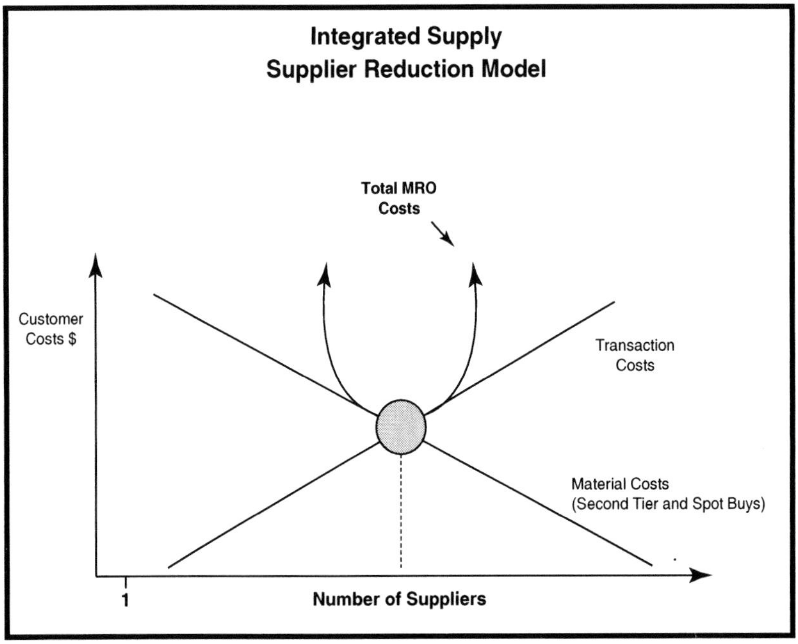

Figure 7.1

However, on the opposite side, suppliers are organized by different commodity groups (Multiple Integrators) and no one supplier can carry all MRO products required. In fact, the material costs for second tier and spot buys go up with fewer suppliers. This is because, at some point, a supplier or a number of suppliers has to go out and second tier source or go out somewhere else to find spot buys. Therefore, the total MRO cost to a customer looks like a "U" curve. When a group of distributors is able to get together and form an alliance or a group that has a consistent approach to the market and has singularity of policies, programs, procedures, technology tools, etc., that group should be able to do over and above a Single Integrator by moving the customer's MRO cost curve down the transaction cost line. In other words, Multiple Integrators who can act and look to the customer as a single supplier, can thereby take advantage of the lower transaction cost per without being adversely influenced by the material costs' curve.

Summary. It is now evident that distributors in general and Multiple and Total Integrators collectively save our companies substantially through process integration and standardization. As manufacturing continues to maximize its own core competencies, distributors are recognized as they were always intended to be: "value adders." Integrated Supply has offered distributors a tremendous opportunity to consolidate itheir customer bases.

Electronic Commerce

Chapter Eight

8.1 Electronic Commerce – The Future is Here

According to a recent survey less than 5% of all companies are actually transacting business on the Internet. Yet by the year 2000 some experts are predicting that the Internet economy will explode into an astounding $200 billion enterprise. In order to participate, organizations must rethink their strategies and priorities as to how to compete in the marketplace. We need to be able to supply the best product to the marketplace at the most competitive rates - and do it faster. The need to improve organizational performance has never been greater. Technological developments over the past few years have led to improvements and cost reductions in computers and communication equipment. With these two processes now integrated, the development of an international computer network and Electronic Commerce has emerged.

Many companies, until recently, have struggled to integrate their computer systems within their own enterprise. Today they are suddenly entering the global arena. With the falling costs of computer hardware and the advent of user-friendly software, businesses are increasingly integrating computers into their processes. The process of linking this technology together to communicate with other computers both inside and outside of the firm is the next logical step in information technology. Telex and fax in the past have proven themselves to be an invaluable business tool, and it is evident that computers are the next largest and logical steps in enhancing the business communications process, both inside and outside the firm.

Electronic Commerce will enable companies to broaden their markets, downsize their supplier bases, attract customers from all over the globe and enter into new business alliances more quickly than ever before.

8.2 What is Electronic Commerce?

Electronic Commerce can be defined as the buying and selling of information, products and services over computer networks. Electronic Commerce differs from traditional procurement methods in the manner in which information is transferred and processed.

Traditionally, commerce is conducted between two individuals who typically use the telephone, mail or fax. In utilizing Electronic Commerce this same information is transferred electronically from computer to computer.

When most people refer to conducting Electronic Commerce, they naturally think only of the buying and selling of products over the Internet. Yet, the Internet is most commonly utilized for consumer-oriented business transactions, and business-to-business transactions. However, Electronic Commerce is not singularly about the buying and selling of product, but also includes:

- Advertising
- Product information
- Invoicing
- Video conferencing
- E-mail
- Debit & credit cards
- Satellite shipment tracking
- Electronic catalogs
- Order status & inquiry
- Payment
- Imaging
- EDI
- Airline reservations

As you can see, there are many ways in which Electronic Commerce can be defined and employed in our business transactions. For the purpose of this book however, Electronic Commerce will be limited to the Internet, Intranet and any other computer to computer transactions such as EDI.

8.3 Advantages in Using Electronic Commerce

Electronic Commerce brings many advantages and benefits while incorporating it into our business strategies. Powerful computers and advanced communications technology have enabled the gathering and processing of information to occur at very rapid speeds. By using this technology we can increase the speed and efficiency in which we conduct our business, enabling us to do business with anyone, anywhere in the world - a global marketplace. These benefits include some of the following:

- Automation of order processes
- Reduced inventory levels
- Reduced overhead
- Improved cycle times/online bidding
- Larger markets/no geographical barrier
- Access to infinite suppliers and customers
- Increased competition
- Local companies can be global
- Immediate response to RFQs and orders

8.4 The Internet

A discussion of Electronic Commerce would not be complete without a discussion about "What is the Internet, anyway?" Most of us have had some exposure, but how does it work? What is its connection to Electronic Commerce?

The Internet is an intricate global electronic communication network of modems and telephone wires connecting computers so that they can share and transfer data and information between each other. The Department of Defense developed the Internet in 1969 to protect defense-sensitive data in case of a nuclear or world-wide attack.

The Internet offers low security and data integrity for sensitive business information; therefore, this has limited its use for business-to-business transactions. The Internet's focus has been on marketing of a product for consumer-oriented activities. International standards for the Internet do not exist, but the system works! It connects all users to a global community and much of it is still uncharted territory to the potential of exchanging business data. During 1996 and 1997, millions of dollars have been spent in the Internet economy. It is imperative that purchasing and materials professionals become 'Internet and Electronic Commerce savvy.' It will be a requirement of a purchaser's future career.

Intranet. This is for internal or end-to-end Web applications to meet departmental, interdepartmental, company-wide or customer–to-supplier connections. Intranet communications can substantially improve productivity between two parties. Because it sits behind a corporate firewall, it appears to be much more secure than a public Web site on the Internet.

8.5 What is the Impact of the Internet on EDI?

For the past two decades many companies have communicated requirements to their key suppliers via Electronic Data Interchange (EDI). However, because of the high cost of entry combined with the technical complications in establishing end-to-end proprietary EDI solutions the growth of this communications medium has been severely limited. The Internet makes EDI a lot less complicated because of its open standards and low cost transmissions. Therefore, instead of investing large funds in developing expensive EDI systems, companies now focus on the more user-friendly, less costly Internet by developing business-to-business Intranet sites. Once security issues have been fully resolved an exodus to private Intranet sites will occur.

8.6 How do Buyers Take Advantage of the Internet?

New Internet users will spend considerable time "surfing the net." Such systems excursions in visiting many supplier Web sites will give them not only a feel for the Internet but also the required confidence and hands-on training. Once familiar with some of the surroundings, buyers will quickly realize that the Internet offers a multitude of opportunities. In particular, locating new suppliers and new products can be very dynamic. Take the following scenario. Pamela, the electronics buyer for a vacuum cleaner manufacturer, received a requisition for a large volume of custom circuit boards. In the past she would have relied on her in-house library and on the Thomas Register catalogs. Today, by using the Internet she called up the Thomas Register on-line and within seconds pulled up several dozen potential sources. From there, Pamela jumped to several supplier Web sites and placed preliminary inquiries while visiting a few of these home pages. This process resulted into the development of an entirely new supplier that has become a major resource to Pamela's company.

Many other purchasing professionals surf the Internet almost daily to look for either new suppliers or new products. By using an Internet search engine such as Yahoo! (www.yahoo.com), the user simply enters a commodity and a flurry of rapid activities result in links to supplier home pages. Because every company can design its own Web page– all companies appear to be the same size. This has leveled the playing field for small companies, as they may appear to be the same in size compared to their larger competitors. Furthermore, the Internet knows of no geographic boundaries, enabling smaller suppliers and foreign competitors to create the perception that they are located nearby.

Listed below are several handy Web sites geared to the purchasing professional:

National Association of Purch. Mgmt: www.napm.org
Purchasing On-line (Purch. Mag.): www.purchasing.com
Thomas Register: www.thomasregister.com
The Whole Internet Catalog: www.nearnet.gnn.com
Elekom Corporation: www.elekom.com
Aquion: www.acquion.com
GE Information Services (GEIS): www.geis.com
W. W. Grainger: www.grainger.com
C. N. Weber Ltd.: www.webersupply.com
SSA Alliance: www.ssalliance.com

All these sites and all others, including international sites, can be visited 24 hours a day, everyday of the year.

8.7 Electronic Catalogs

Initially most companies used Web pages to advertise their products. Today, however many suppliers and distributors have developed extensive electronic catalogs complete with product pictures, specifications and order placement methods. The primary suppliers of such electronic catalogs are Acquion, Elekom and Geis (GE Information Systems). Software enhancements have been developed that make the order release process from these catalogs fully integrated whereby the buyer can release an order via the Internet without also having to open a separate purchase order within his own system. This has been accomplished by interfacing the electronic catalog with the customer's systems legend such as SAP, Oracle, SSA BPCS and Baan among others.

Acquion offers different Internet-based services such as:

SITE: This public Web site has been designed as an economical way for buyers and sellers of commodities of surplus materials to connect globally on a real-time basis. This site provides for bid management, auction and bidding lists and bulletin boards.

BASE: This is also a public Web site enabling buyers to select and release RFQs and purchase orders from an extensive catalog product offering.

GETS: This is a private Intranet site between the buyer and the seller with electronic capabilities as provided by this electronic catalog house. All products and pricing have been prenegotiated.

Elekom offers, in addition to electronic catalog capabilities, an entire fully integrated procurement system with end-to-end integration of every activity between employees and suppliers. The Internet is used for supplier catalog maintenance while the system's open architecture facilitates integration with other business applications.

GEIS offers global network solutions including EDI and messaging services, Internet and Intranet services, and a full suite of applications that help streamline Supply Chain Management processes.

8.8 Why Utilize Electronic Commerce?

The pace of change in business has never been greater than it is today. These changes are driven by improvements in technology, world-wide communications and the removal of trade barriers. The access and speed provided by the Internet alone have opened a large window of opportunity for growth in business. In order to take advantage of the Internet, we must become systems savvy and at the same time make it part of our business strategy. From a procurement point of view this includes not just "surfing the net" and placing orders over this new medium but an entirely different approach toward the way we think in terms of the entire process. This again means developing processes by linking the customers (requisitioners) and suppliers.

Once fully comfortable with the Internet, purchasing professionals can develop their own Web site as a marketing tool in attracting new suppliers. To a large degree the Web site can take the place of welcome booklets, and is also an opportunity to communicate Purchasing's mission, policies, and rules on minority business and other issues. Some new sites even include an electronic supplier survey, which allows for initial screening by asking the supplier for information such as the products it produces, its market-share, capacity utilization and other strategic issues. Establishing a Web site can also help Purchasing manage other responsibilities under its jurisdiction such as managing waste, scrap, and other manufacturing by-products. Well-known companies with a Purchasing Web site include: Sony, Brother International, Reynolds Metals, Hitachi, Siemens, Toshiba and many others.

8.9 Security on the Internet

Even though all major banks do business on the Internet, horror stories keep erupting on the safety and security of the

Internet. Most procurement professionals are still not prepared to send financial and confidential information over the Internet. Network security usually begins with a "firewall," a combination of hardware and software designed to form a boundary between companies inside the network and the rest of the Internet. However, no company is an island, at least not if the company wants to exchange information with its trading partners.

The major security issues include:

- Confidentiality – each transaction to remain private
- Data Integrity – the document remains unaltered
- Authentication – the recipient can be sure of the identity of the sender
- Nonrepudiation – the sender cannot credibly deny sending the document

Until these security issues can be worked out, the Internet will remain a consumer- and Public-Sector-driven entity. Intranet transactions, however, will continue to skyrocket in both transactions and revenues generated.

Acknowledgments:

Brooker, Dena, *Modern Purchasing,* Toronto, Ontario.

Caffrey, Brian G. , Jenny Martin C.P.M., A.P.P., Roland Rugoletti, C.P.M. and Dee Smith. "Electronic Commerce: Putting Information Technology to Work," *NAPM 82nd Annual International Conference Proceedings,* Washington D.C. 1997.

Carr, Jeffrey, "Electronic Commerce: Is This the Future State of Supply?" *82nd Annual International Purchasing Conference,* Washington D.C. 1997.

Harari, Liat and Dalit Tzafrir, "Electronic Commerce," WWW.

Hollar, Rick S. "Pick a Card, Any Card," *Purchasing Today,* June 1997.

Krostseng, Lee C.P.M. "Should My Organization's Purchasing Department Have a Web Site?" *P.M. News,* June 1997.

Minaham, Tim, *Purchasing Magazine,* June 1997.

Raedels, Dr. Alan C.P.M. and Dr. Lee Buddress, C.P.M. Portland State University Portland, Oregon.

Schaaf, Dick, "Just the FAQs: Using Intranets for Training," *Training,* June 1997.

Steggell, Dan C.P.M., A.P.P., CPIM, "Becoming an E-Commerce Champion," *Purchasing Today,* June 1997.

"What is Electronic Commerce?" *EC net, The Electronic Commerce Information Resource, Year-X Ltd.* Web Site, 1996.

RESOURCE GUIDE

ADDITIONAL PURCHASING RESOURCES FROM PT PUBLICATIONS, INC.

3109 45th Street, Suite 100
West Palm Beach, FL 33407-1915
1-800-547-4326

THE PURCHASING ENCYCLOPEDIA

Just-In-Time Purchasing: In Pursuit of Excellence $29.95
Peter L. Grieco, Jr., Michael W. Gozzo
& Jerry W. Claunch

Glossary of Key Purchasing Terms, Acronyms, and Formulas PT Publications	$14.95
Supplier Certification II: A Handbook for Achieving Excellence through Continuous Improvement Peter L. Grieco, Jr.	$49.95
World Class: Measuring Its Achievement Peter L. Grieco, Jr.	$39.95
Purchasing Performance Measurements: A Roadmap For Excellence Mel Pilachowski	$12.95
The World Of Negotiations: Never Being a Loser Peter L. Grieco, Jr. and Paul G. Hine	$39.95
How To Conduct Supplier Surveys and Audits Janet L. Przirembel	$14.95
Supply Management Toolbox: How to Manage Your Suppliers Peter L. Grieco, Jr.	$26.95
Purchasing Capital Equipment Thomas E. Petroski	$14.95
Power Purchasing: Supply Management in in the 21st Century Peter L. Grieco, Jr. and Carl R. Cooper	$39.95
Global Sourcing Lee Krotseng	$14.95
Purchasing Contract Law, UCC, and Patents Mark Grieco	$14.95
EDI Purchasing: The Electronic Gateway to the Future Steven Marks	$14.95
Leasing Smart Craig A. Melby and Jane Utzman	$14.95
MRO Purchasing Peter L. Grieco, Jr.	$14.95

The Complete Guide to Contracts Management For Facilities Services John P. Mahoney and Linda S. Keckler	$18.95
Purchasing Transportation D. J. "Jack" Scalera, III	$14.95
Purchasing Ethics Peter L. Grieco, Jr.	$14.95
Supplier Selection Judith A. Stimson	$14.95
Supply Chain Management Peter L. Grieco, Jr. and John Gossmann	$14.95

PURCHASING VIDEO EDUCATION SERIES

Supplier Certification The Path to Excellence

Tape 1: Why Supplier Certification?	$395.00
Tape 2: Quality at the Supplier	$395.00
Tape 3: How to Select a Supplier	$395.00
Tape 4: Supplier Surveys and Audits	$395.00
Tape 5: Supplier Quality Agreements	$395.00
Tape 6: Supplier Ratings	$395.00
Tape 7: Phases of Supplier Certification	$395.00
Tape 8: Implementing a Supplier Cert. Program	$395.00
Tape 9: Evaluating Your Supplier Cert. Program	$395.00
Complete Nine Tape Series	$1,995.00

PURCHASING AUDIO TAPES

The World of Negotiations: How to Win Every Time	$39.95

PURCHASING SOFTWARE

Supplier Survey and Audit Software Developed by Professionals For Technology, Inc.	$395.00

ADDITIONAL PROFESSIONAL TEXTBOOKS

Failure Modes and Effects Analysis: Predicting and Preventing Problems Before They Occur Paul Palady	$39.95
Made In America: The Total Business Concept Peter L. Grieco, Jr. and Michael W. Gozzo	$29.95
Reengineering Through Cycle Time Management Wayne L. Douchkoff and Thomas E. Petroski	$39.95
Behind Bars: Bar Coding Principles and Applications Peter L. Grieco, Jr., Michael W. Gozzo and C.J. Long	$39.95
People Empowerment: Achieving Success from Involvement Michael W. Gozzo and Wayne L. Douchkoff	$39.95
Activity Based Costing: The Key to World Class Performance Peter L. Grieco, Jr. and Mel Pilachowski	$18.00
Set Up Reduction: The Next Millenium Thomas E. Petroski	$26.95

INDEX

A

B

C